Bud E. Smith

Sams **Teach Yourself**

Facebook®
for Business

in **10 Minutes**

SAMS

Indiana 46240

Sams Teach Yourself Facebook® for Business in 10 Minutes
Copyright © 2011 by Pearson Education, Inc.

ISBN-13: 978-0-672-33555-6
ISBN-10: 0-672-33555-7

Library of Congress Cataloging-in-Publication Data:

Smith, Bud E.
  Sams teach yourself Facebook for business in 10 minutes / Bud E. Smith.
     p. cm.
  Includes bibliographical references and index.
  ISBN-13: 978-0-672-33555-6 (alk. paper)
  ISBN-10: 0-672-33555-7
  1. Facebook (Electronic resource) 2. Online social networks. 3. Social networks—Computer network resources. 4. Web sites—Design. I. Title.
  HM743.F33S65 2011
  006.7'54—dc22

                                          2011009991

Printed in the United States of America

First Printing June 2011

Trademarks

All terms mentioned in this book that are known to be trademarks or service marks have been appropriately capitalized. Pearson Education, Inc. cannot attest to the accuracy of this information. Use of a term in this book should not be regarded as affecting the validity of any trademark or service mark.

Warning and Disclaimer

Bulk Sales

Pearson Education, Inc. offers excellent disc when ordered in quantity for bulk purchases more information, please contact

   U.S. Corporate and Government Sales
   1-800-382-3419
   corpsales@pearsontechgroup.com

For sales outside of the U.S., please contac

   International Sales
   international@pearson.com

Editor-in-Chief
Greg Wiegand

Executive Editor
Rick Kughen

Development Editor
Mark Reddin

Managing Editor
Kristy Hart

Project Editor
Anne Goebel

Copy Editor
Language Logistics, LLC

Senior Indexer
Cheryl Lenser

Technical Editor
Karen Weinstein

Publishing Coordinator
Cindy Teeters

Book Designer
Anne Jones

Compositor
Nonie Ratcliff

Contents at a Glance

Table of Contents

About the Author

Bud Smith is one of the leading computer book authors working today. He began writing computer books back in 1984, the year of the iconic 1984 television commercial for the Macintosh. Bud has written and edited guides to buying computers, books about using all kinds of software, and doing almost anything you can think of online. His books have sold more than a million copies.

One noteworthy recent title is *Sams Teach Yourself Google Places in 10 Minutes*, a detailed description of how to use the new, free Google advertising service. Bud has written extensively about online business and new mobile devices, with titles including *Sams Teach Yourself Apple iPad in 10 Minutes*, *WordPress in Depth*, and *Internet Marketing For Dummies*.

Bud continues to work as a writer, project manager, and marketer to help people get the most out of advancing technology. He currently lives in the San Francisco Bay area, participating in environmental causes when he's not working on technology-related projects.

Dedication

To James, who got on the Facebook rocket ship early and helped steer it toward the stars.

Acknowledgments

The first person to thank is Rick Kughen, who quickly "got" the opportunity for a book about Facebook from the business side; to development editor Mark Reddin for helping bring the first mainstream book about Facebook for Business into being; to copy editor Chrissy White for helping straighten snarled syntax; to technical editor Karen Weinstein for making sure everything said here is true and correct; and finally to the production team at Pearson, who applied their talents to bring my musings about using Facebook for business purposes into the attractive and useful *Teach Yourself* format.

We Want to Hear from You!

As the reader of this book, *you* are our most important critic and commentator. We value your opinion and want to know what we're doing right, what we could do better, what areas you'd like to see us publish in, and any other words of wisdom you're willing to pass our way.

You can email or write me directly to let me know what you did or didn't like about this book—as well as what we can do to make our books stronger.

Please note that I cannot help you with technical problems related to the topic of this book, and that due to the high volume of mail I receive, I might not be able to reply to every message.

When you write, please be sure to include this book's title and author as well as your name and phone or email address. I will carefully review your comments and share them with the author and editors who worked on the book.

E-mail: consumer@samspublishing.com

Mail: Greg Wiegand
         Editor-in-Chief
         Sams Publishing
         800 East 96th Street
         Indianapolis, IN 46240 USA

Reader Services

Visit our website and register this book at informit.com/register for convenient access to any updates, downloads, or errata that might be available for this book.

Introduction

Facebook is the biggest online phenomenon of recent years. With more than 500 million—yes, that's half a billion—users, and growing, Facebook's pageviews rival those of fellow Web leader Google. Facebook has re-united old flames, helped people make new and keep existing friends, and kept families in touch across great distances.

Facebook is all about connecting people. It's a new way to keep in touch—easier than meeting in person or a phone call, but richer and more personal than many email or text message exchanges. People young enough to have used Facebook in high school and college are more likely to stay in touch with their classmates after graduation, for instance, than earlier generations.

Now, Facebook has added new features that make it a potent tool for business. These tools include Facebook Places, which allows people to "check in" to a specific place on a mobile device; Facebook Deals, which can reward you for checking in to a place; and Facebook Ads, which are said to often be much more cost-effective than the Google equivalent.

Facebook has also improved fan pages—pages controlled by a business, organization, or well-known individual. The owner of a fan page can comment, like other fan pages, and interact much like an individual user of Facebook. This opens the door to a whole new way to stay connected to your customers.

After being founded at Harvard at the turn of the century, Facebook just grew and grew. A movie about Facebook founder Mark Zuckerberg, called The Social Network, is a big hit, and former Alaska governor Sarah Palin has used her Facebook page as a major political platform, although not without criticism. "Friending" people and "liking" Web pages have moved beyond Facebook to become commonplaces in people's conversations. Facebook games like Farmville have become widely popular.

For established businesses to crack Facebook, though, has been tricky. Facebook's somewhat bland user interface makes branding difficult. Some business Facebook pages "go viral" and get hundreds of thousands of "likes," while others, which might appear just as promising, get none.

Even as business has somewhat languished on Facebook, Google has pioneered new ways for businesses to make, and spend, money online. Google AdWords, which allows companies to publish ads (mostly small, text ads) on Google search results pages, has made tens of billions of dollars a year for Google.

Google Places is a newer feature that allows companies to have a local presence in Google Search and Google Maps. Google Places includes easy-to-use coupons.

Facebook has followed with its own offering using the same name, Facebook Places, and the much more invitingly named Facebook Deals. Neither is really all that different than the Google equivalent. The difference in how much good they are for you mostly has to do with the difference between Facebook and Google.

The driving force behind Google is searching, leading to the rise of search engine optimization (SEO) and the way AdWords ties search terms to ad placements to ad clickthroughs. The driving force behind Facebook, though, is the "social graph"—the online links between Facebook users and their Facebook-using friends, families, and work colleagues. On Facebook, it's all about connecting.

On Facebook, of course, everyone you're connected to is a "friend." You can put friends into different groups, but not that many people do.

Google works well when you're targeting the individual searcher looking for something specific. Facebook works well when you want to "tip" a group of Facebook friends into becoming customers. The Facebook effort is harder, because you're trying to get groups of people to come together. But a "win" that you achieve through Facebook advertising can be very powerful indeed.

On Facebook, you start with a Places page and a fan page. You can combine them, which Facebook recommends, or keep them separate, which I think is generally better. Then, on your Places page or combined page, you offer Facebook Deals. Getting people to take advantage of Deals may not be the only purpose of your Facebook advertising campaign, but it's the best measurement of its overall success.

Part of the way you "win" new business through Facebook is quite challenging. You have to help people feel comfortable with your Facebook presence. That includes well-written copy, interesting images, and compelling special offers. But it also means understanding how people work, how they see your company and your products, and how they use Facebook within their lives.

For text ads, at least, Google AdWords advertising is a bit like an engineering project. You can try dozens of variations and test the effectiveness of each, one user at a time.

Effective Facebook advertising, though, requires that people recommend your offer to their friends. Attracting Facebook users includes subjective factors, and is more like making a great TV commercial. Everything you do has to be "right"—copy, images, layout, spelling—just to get people to pay attention. But there's room for creative flair to make the difference between failure (not earning back your investment), moderate success, and a runaway hit advertising campaign.

Use this book to put together effective Facebook Places pages, fan pages, and Deals. Work hard, and monitor your results. Then, when you've got the basics down, start brainstorming on top of the solid base you've built. Add some fun and liveliness to your Facebook presence, and hope for magic to happen.

About This Book

This book really delves into the business uses of Facebook; as far as using Facebook goes, there's only a brief overview of Facebook basics here. If you need an introductory guide to get you warmed up, start with *Sams Teach Yourself Facebook in 10 Minutes*. Create a personal Facebook page and get some experience with making Facebook friends, so you know what's going on.

As part of the Sams Teach Yourself in 10 Minutes series of guides, this book aims to teach you the ins and outs of using Facebook for business, without using up a lot of your precious time. Divided into easy-to-follow lessons that you can tackle in about 10 minutes each, you learn the following Facebook tasks and topics:

▶ Setting up your personal Facebook profile

▶ Finding and installing apps

▶ Creating a Facebook fan page for your business

▶ Claiming your Facebook Places page

▶ Combining your business and Places pages—or not

▶ Editing your Places page

▶ Supporting multiple locations

▶ Driving traffic to your Places page

▶ Creating Facebook Deals

▶ Creating Facebook Ads

▶ Budgeting for Facebook Ads

▶ Tracking the impact of your Facebook presence

After you finish these lessons, and the others in this book, you'll know all you need to know to take Facebook for your business as far as you want it to go.

Who This Book Is For

This book is aimed at all business owners, or leaders of other kinds of organizations, who want to create a Facebook fan page for their business, who want to have a Places page and Deals, who want to do Facebook advertising—or all of the above. This should mean just about everyone in business, or working in an organization!

You may have extensive computer and online experience, or you may have very little. You may also have some experience in marketing your business or organization through various means, including print and/or online media, or you may have very little marketing background as well. This book will help you succeed on Facebook—whatever that means to you.

Throughout this book, the term "business owners" is meant very broadly. If you work in a social services agency, a public facility such as a swimming pool, or a nonprofit, you have people who you might call "clients," "customers," or some other term. They still need to know about what you're offering and how to take advantage of it. So "business" isn't just about for-profit businesses. (Though I like profits, too.) It means any store, location, or service provider that's open to the public!

Each lesson in this book focuses on one specific topic, such as creating your Facebook Places page or creating a Deal that's attractive to your online visitors. You can skip from one topic to another, read the book through from start to finish, or both. You can hand it to a friend, family member, or colleague to answer a specific question that they have, too.

What Do I Need to Use This Book?

You will need a computer with a web browser and reliable Internet access to use this book. A tablet computer, such as the iPad, or a small, low-cost netbook will probably not be adequate for the tasks needed; you will probably want either a Windows PC or a Macintosh. Either a desktop or a laptop model will do the job.

If you are not experienced with computers, or don't have a computer, you may wish to buy a computer and procure Internet access, then learn how to use the computer itself and a web browser before proceeding.

Alternatively, you can find a friend or work colleague with the necessary equipment and skills and get their help in carrying out the tasks involved. If you are the one with the necessities, you can provide help to others; it's fun to work together on tasks such as those involved with a Facebook presence.

Conventions Used in This Book

Whenever you need to push a particular button on your computer, or click
a particular control onscreen, you'll find the label or name for that item
bolded in the text, such as "click the **Home** button." In addition to the text
and figures in this book, you'll also encounter some special boxes labelled
Tip, Note, or Caution.

> TIP
>
> Tips offer helpful shortcuts or easier ways to do something.

> NOTE
>
> Notes are extra bits of information related to the text that might
> help you expand your knowledge or understanding.

> CAUTION
>
> Cautions are warnings or other important information you need to
> know about the consequences of using a feature or executing a
> task.

Screen Captures

Most of the figures captured for this book come from a Windows PC running Internet Explorer 8 and showing various web pages, mostly Facebook
pages of various sorts. A few of the screenshots are from an Apple iPad
running Apple's Safari web browser. You might use a Macintosh, or a
Windows PC running a different version of Windows than what is shown
in this book.

You may use a different web browser than we show in this book, or a
different version of Internet Explorer, and different settings for your
computer and your web browser. You may well also use a different mobile
device than the iPad. For any of these reasons, your screens may look
somewhat different than those in the book. Also keep in mind that the

developers of Facebook and the software and other websites shown in this book are constantly working to improve their software, websites, and the services offered on them.

New features are added regularly to the Windows and MacOS, software, and websites, and old features change or disappear. This means the screen contents change often, so your own screens may differ from the screens shown in this book. Don't be too alarmed, however. The basics, though they are tweaked in appearance from time to time, stay mostly the same in principle and usage.

LESSON 1

Introducing Facebook for Business

In this lesson, you learn why Facebook is so popular, and why your business should be part of the Facebook phenomenon. You learn the differences between a personal Facebook Page and a business Facebook Page, and see how one large business uses Facebook.

Why Facebook Is So Popular

Facebook is amazingly popular. It started out at Harvard as "The Facebook," an online version of the printed "face books" that some universities use to help new students meet each other. Facebook then spread to other universities.

For a long time, you could only join Facebook if you had an email address showing you were a student at a designated Facebook university—mzuckerberg@harvard.edu, for instance. And the focus was local; the goal was interacting online with other students at your school, who you would also see in person as you attended classes, went to parties, and so on. As Facebook grew, some of that local focus was lost.

In using Facebook for business, many businesses will want to re-introduce that same kind of local focus. Your Facebook fan page for your business can have a local focus. Facebook Places and Deals, which I describe later in this book, help you do that, and Facebook Ads can be geo-targeted—that is, only shown to people in a specific city, town, or area.

Targeting your Facebook presence is important precisely because of just how extensive Facebook has become. With more than 500 million users, Facebook is everywhere. Half of Facebook's users log in every day, and active users check it dozens of times a day. Figure 1.1 shows a map of the world, drawn by connecting a random sample of about 10 million Facebook friends and their locations.

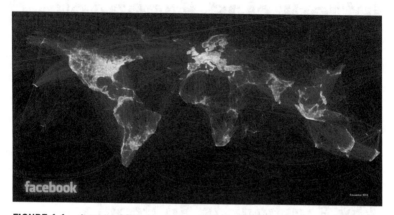

FIGURE 1.1   A map of Facebook friends lights up almost the entire world.

Facebook has become so popular because it is very personal and entirely global at the same time. Every person who joins Facebook helps pull other people onto it and increases the loyalty of their real-world friends, who now become Facebook friends as well. This kind of growth, where each new user makes the whole service more valuable, is called the "network effect" in computing and marketing theory.

NOTE: **A Facebook Friends Map Lights Up the World**

In addition to being beautiful, the Facebook friends map gives some idea of Facebook's extensive reach—and shows the areas that Facebook has not yet penetrated as deeply. (Brazil, for instance, still has many millions of fans of Orkut, a rival social network owned by Google.) To see the map and the explanation behind it for yourself, search for "Visualizing Friendships" on Facebook.

Facebook is more "everywhere" in some places than others. The United States, Canada, and the UK are thoroughly "Facebooked." Three out of four American Web users are on Facebook, but of course not everyone is equally active. An infographic available at Mashable.com, shown in Figure

1.2, has some interesting and useful facts. Visit: http://mashable.com/2011/
01/12/obsessed-with-facebook-infographic/.

FIGURE 1.2   Mashable.com has a fun and useful Facebook infographic.

France, Germany, and Italy are not far behind North America and the UK.
In all these countries, almost everyone under 30 entered adulthood with a
Facebook account and with Facebook as an active part of their social lives.
Some of these people are such strong Facebook users that they hardly use
email anymore, at least outside of the workplace, because Facebook takes
care of most of their personal messaging needs.

In other countries, and among people over 30, Facebook is used and
understood differently. It's still somewhat of an enthusiast's tool, popular

in some social circles and not others. The very word "Facebook" carries a different weight for these different audiences.

For this reason, Facebook is almost never the whole answer for your online marketing needs. You absolutely need Facebook to reach some groups, such as current college students; but you have to use other tools, such as Google, to reach others.

> **NOTE: What Would Google Do?**
> Google has pioneered online marketing tools and makes most of its money—tens of billions of dollars a year—from AdWords ads alone. To some extent, Facebook is playing catch-up to Google, but it's doing so in a way that shows a deep understanding of how people actually use Facebook. Facebook Places and Deals and Facebook Ads are a newer and better way for reaching active Facebook users than their Google equivalents. Facebook fan pages aren't matched by Google at all. See my books, *Sams Teach Yourself Google Places in 10 Minutes* and *Teach Yourself Google AdWords in 10 Minutes*, for details on Google's offering. This book covers about the same range of material as my two Google-related books taken together. (How? Practice makes perfect, I guess...)

If you didn't grow up with Facebook, you might not "get it" in the same way as the people who did grow up with it. That's OK; this book will help you use Facebook competently for your business. You should definitely use Facebook, though, in your personal life—set up a personal Profile page, "friend" people, "like" businesses that treat you well, and so on. Using Facebook in your personal life will help you do a much better job of investing your precious time and money wisely in using Facebook for business.

Why Your Business Should Be on Facebook

The fact that something is popular doesn't mean your business has to use it. However, Facebook is moving from "popular" to "ubiquitous";

depending on where your business is and who your customers are, Facebook is part of daily life for many, or even the majority, of your customers.

> CAUTION: **The Comma Police Are Watching**
> Many Facebook users are quite careless about spelling and punctuation, but you can't afford to be. For content that represents your business, do whatever it takes to make sure it is "clean" and correct. Even on your personal Facebook Page, you should make your contributions close to perfect in spelling, grammar, punctuation and so on, because that will make your business look fully professional.

There's also a competitive element to this. Eventually, most businesses are going to be on Facebook. In general, the longer you wait to get on Facebook, the more "out of it" your business will seem to heavy Facebook users. And if your competitors make a showing on Facebook before you do, they'll get the early "buzz" among Facebook users and gain momentum that you'll be hard pressed to catch up with.

Consider a local bookstore. Every local bookstore competes with Amazon.com, and Amazon has more than 500,000 Facebook fans at this point (that is, people who've clicked the Like button on Amazon's Facebook Page, as shown in Figure 1.3).

Half a million is a huge number of people, but it's only one out of 1,000 Facebook users in the area that Amazon serves—most of the world. To match Amazon's penetration of its target market, a local bookstore just has to get one out of 1,000 Facebook users in the area *it* serves.

The area I live in, the Rockridge area of Oakland, has about 20,000 people. So getting just 20 Facebook fans would be a good start for a local bookstore—and might just beat Amazon within that neighborhood. The first local bookstore to "beat Amazon" in this way would get strong momentum with local Facebook users and might go on to get hundreds of Facebook fans. Among local bookstores, they'll be known as "the one on Facebook." Bookstores that try the same thing later will probably find it harder to get traction.

FIGURE 1.3   Amazon has a huge reach on Facebook, but you can beat them locally.

NOTE: **Start Your Website with a Facebook Page**

What if you don't have a website yet? To start out, you probably should. The Web as a whole has many more users than Facebook, and not being on the Web makes it hard for some of your customers to consider you fully. So should you drop this book and go create a website? Not at all. Creating a Facebook fan page for your business, or even a Places page, is easier than creating a stand-alone web page. So start on Facebook first and then create a website, using what you learn on Facebook. You'll save time and money.

In fact, Facebook might be more valuable to a local bookstore than it is to Amazon. That's because a local bookstore can take advantage of its local knowledge. Amazon's fan page has to be somewhat generic, addressing the whole world. A local bookstore can use its knowledge of local concerns, local issues, and local events to reach its customers and their Facebook friends.

This ties into two advantages of Facebook: hypertargeting, and connections to social networks. You can target your Facebook presence to reach very specific audiences. And you can reach into people's networks of friends, family members, and co-workers. Once you get a couple of key influencers in a group of friends to, say, come to an event that you're sponsoring, the rest may well follow.

Here's a brief, targeted list of the key reasons you and your business should be on Facebook:

- ▶ **To reach people.** Your Facebook fan page can reach many of your customers, particularly those 30 and under. Simply having them see your business on Facebook will help you stay connected with them.

- ▶ **To make money.** You can use Facebook Places and Deals to actually bring people into your physical location, call you, order online—however you do business. It's easy to measure the results of these efforts and to justify just the effort you put in.

- ▶ **To not be left out.** Every time someone looks for your business on Facebook and can't find it, that's a negative for you. If they then look for a competitor and do find them instead, it's a bigger negative for you.

- ▶ **For positive "buzz."** Just the fact that people know you're on Facebook is a positive, even if they're not fans (that is, they haven't "Liked" your fan page). There's so much positive momentum around Facebook in the press and among ordinary people that simply associating yourself with Facebook is a plus. If you can get your Facebook presence mentioned in online comments and even the print press, as many businesses have, all the better.

A word of caution, though—some of this impact can be measured, but not all of it can. Just as you probably don't have precise numbers for how many people know about your business or what people think of it, you won't be able to precisely measure all of the impact of being (or not being) on Facebook.

However, because Facebook has gotten so big, it's an easy call—you need to join in! Then you can use measurable efforts such as Facebook Deals to help determine just how hard you work at developing and using your Facebook presence.

TIP: **Use Facebook to Get in the Press**

The press is always looking for "local color" on a national or global story, or industry-specific color on a general business story. And they're always writing about Facebook. So get press people to "Like" your Facebook fan page and keep them up to date on your online presence. They may very well cite your business in a story, or even come to you for a quote when they're on deadline. Such mentions can be very valuable to your business.

Comparing Personal and Business Facebook Pages

Your Facebook business presence has a number of moving parts, which all relate to each other. This book's lessons go into detail on all of them. The following is a brief look at the concept of a personal Facebook Page, and then a popular business fan page is dissected in comparison.

Your Personal Facebook Page

You should have a personal Facebook Page before creating a business Facebook presence. Why? Because it's very difficult to create an effective Facebook business presence if you don't know how Facebook works for its users. In fact, if you're not a user yourself, you may well make "tone deaf" mistakes in how you present your business online.

NOTE: **The Facebook Presence**

If you have little previous Facebook experience, you might want to stop here and create a personal Facebook Page. I give a brief tour in Lesson 2, "Setting Up a Business-Friendly Profile Page," but you'll probably need something more in-depth to really do it right. *Sams Teach Yourself Facebook in 10 Minutes* is exactly targeted to help get you going as a Facebook user.

A Facebook personal page is shown in Figure 1.4. If you use Facebook, you probably already know that what you're seeing here is the Wall, which is available under the Profile tab. It's made up of postings that you create, and it's what other people see when they first visit you.

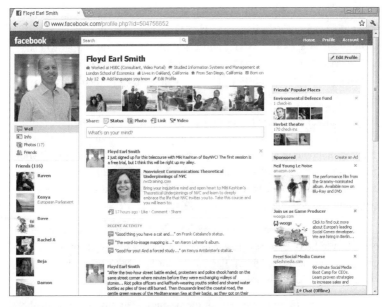

FIGURE 1.4   Your Facebook Wall shows what you post.

Confusingly, what you usually see when using Facebook is your News Feed. Basically, the News Feed is little bits and pieces of updates from other people—which show up on their Walls—all mixed together. To see what you're putting out to the world, visit your own Wall regularly.

It's also worth knowing that not all of your Facebook friends see everything you post. Facebook keeps track of who responds to whom, who visits each other's Walls, and so on—and prioritizes what shows up in people's News Feeds accordingly. If your Facebook friends are already well involved on Facebook, it might be hard to get them to see your Facebook postings, and if they don't respond, you may drop off their News Feeds again.

This is true for the default part of the News Feed, called Top News. If you click Most Recent, you see all the updates. Not many people know to do this though. Also, for many people, the volume of posts in Most Recent is overwhelming, so they stick with Top News.

To get connected with updates on Top News, visit the Walls of key friends. (Look them up in Facebook using the Search bar, or click to them from within your Friends list.) You might want to follow up on people whose updates you aren't seeing once a week or so. To further establish contact, message people whose posts you aren't seeing—they probably aren't seeing yours either.

This has direct relevance to your business presence, too. (Again, part of the reason you need a personal Facebook presence is to understand what might be happening with your business presence.) People can "Like" your business presence, but if you and they don't engage further, your business can drop off their radar within their use of Facebook. So you'll want to take steps to keep engagement up.

Another tricky question on Facebook is about how much your personal page should be tied to—or perhaps even restricted by—your business presence. Your personal Facebook Page and your Facebook friendships, "Likes," and so on will reflect on the business.

The same goes for all employees of the business, but not as much for the more junior ones. If a retail clerk who's the employee of a small business, for example, posts on Facebook about his wild weekend, some potential customers might look negatively on the business as a whole based on the association. This is a tricky area and probably best handled simply by pointing it out to people, or giving them training classes in the proper use of Facebook.

As you use your personal Facebook Page, keep an eye on what appeals to you, what you enjoy, and what annoys you. This will help you decide what to do for your business presence. Talk to employees, colleagues, and friends about this, too. You'll avoid lots of potential mistakes and get solid ideas for things you can do to help improve your Facebook business presence.

TIP: **Changes to Groups**

Facebook Groups used to be a kind of Facebook mailing list that was tied to your personal page. The old Groups were potentially useful for business. Recently, though, Groups have been redesigned, and are now more a way to "target" your Facebook postings separately to friends, family, co-workers and so on. There isn't a huge business relevance to your use of the new Groups. However, you can use Groups to restrict your comments about how much fun you had at your bachelor (or bachelorette) party to a small group, rather than broadcasting them to everyone. This can help you and others associated with your business to keep your business and work lives separate, but it is somewhat of a pain. And don't use obscenities, slander people, post embarrassing photos, discuss anything illegal, and so on, no matter how limited you think the distribution is.

Examining a Facebook Fan Page for Business

Facebook started calling pages that represent organizations "fan" pages because they were first used by fans of musicians, actors, and so on. Now, though, Facebook simply calls them Facebook Pages, which is confusing. You'll still hear the "fan" language used to describe Facebook Pages, though, and I use it here, because it's widely used and easy to understand.

The Amazon Facebook page is very simple, which makes it a good example for any business just starting out with a Facebook Page. However, Amazon has done a couple of things to make the page work well for them.

When you first visit the Amazon.com Facebook Page, you don't go to the Wall, as you normally would. Instead, Amazon has specified that new users go to the Welcome tab, shown in Figure 1.5. Note that the Welcome tab contains a blatant invitation to "Like" the page and that it makes a promise: You'll get early access to "deals, news and exclusive content." This is a great example of a tactic to consider using in your own business.

FIGURE 1.5   Amazon really, really wants you to "Like" them.

As I mentioned previously in this lesson, people who "Like" the page are likely to see updates from Amazon on their News Feeds. However, if they never interact with Amazon again, the updates may drop off. So the information that Amazon sends has to get people engaged so that the brand stays in people's Facebook world.

Most people, after either Liking or not Liking the page, will then go to the Wall. Figure 1.6 shows Amazon's Facebook Wall and highlights some of the major elements.

> ▶ **Updates.** Amazon's Wall shows updates and links posted to the page. These updates show up on the News Feeds of people who "Like" the Amazon.com Facebook Page. As shown in Figure 1.6,

and as you'll see if you visit the page yourself, it's strictly business. Enthusiastic and upbeat, yes, but all about business.

▶ **Big logo.** Amazon uses a big logo. It suggests movement— probably wanting Facebook users to "move" to the Amazon.com site and buy a book.

▶ **Fans/Likes.** On a person's status page, there's a link to their list of Friends; on a business Facebook Page, there's a list of people who Like the page.

▶ **Favorite pages.** For both a business and a personal page, this is where you show something about yourself through your affiliations.

FIGURE 1.6   The Amazon Facebook Page is simple.

▶ **Tabs (links to major sections).** I go into more detail about tabs in Lesson 9, "Claiming Your Places Page," which discusses Facebook Places. Amazon.com has the traditional Info tab, which tells you something about the business. It also has added a tab for their Twitter feed about deals, @amazondeals; a Welcome tab; a Careers tab for job-seekers, which is appropriate given Facebook's young audience; Support, which just links into web pages on Amazon.com; and a Photos tab.

> TIP: **Avoiding Too Many Tabs**
>
> The major categories of a website are called "tabs," even if they're links on the side of the page, which is what you see with Facebook fan pages. Try not to have too many tabs. The average person can remember four to seven things in short-term memory at once, and that's a good guideline for the number of tabs you should limit yourself to.

Note that there are no apps or ads cluttering up the area to the right—called the "right-hand rail" in web design. Instead, there's just one solitary promotion from Facebook that encourages people to create a page, as I describe in Lesson 3, "Finding and Installing Apps."

Understanding How a Big Business Uses Facebook

Amazon uses its Facebook fan page for "presence" on Facebook. They don't sell on Facebook, nor interact heavily with their fans. A "presence" is a worthy initial goal for your Facebook fan page, too. Amazon management can proudly say, "We're on Facebook." The Amazon Facebook fan page delivers a steady stream of relevant, though somewhat boring, information. The deals are great, but there's not a lot of warmth, humor, or human interest.

Amazon also uses their Facebook presence to tie together their Twitter stream, the support pages on their website, the Careers pages on their website, and photos. Their main goal looks to be to use the power of their brand to get an impressive number of Likes—which, of course, will help further build the power of their brand.

What Amazon is not doing on Facebook, at least so far, is building up any kind of local presence or encouraging discussion. Amazon is not, of course, a local business, so that avenue is largely closed. Your business may be much more strongly local, and Facebook is great for that, both in the content you and others contribute, which can have a strong local flavor, and in using Facebook Deals and Ads to geo-target your spending.

Amazon is also not targeting people's social networks, and this may be a missed opportunity. People feel passionately about books, but also about other products, such as favorite video cameras. Facebook is great for building communities around these kinds of topics, which can have your business at the center. If you can use your Facebook presence to tap into existing social networks, you may be able to beat Amazon, and your direct competitors, at their own game!

Summary

In this lesson, you learned why Facebook is so popular, and why your business should be part of the Facebook phenomenon. You learned the differences between a personal Facebook Page and a business Facebook Page, and saw how one large business uses Facebook. In the next lesson, you learn how to set up your personal Profile page in a business-friendly way.

LESSON 2

Setting Up a Business-Friendly Profile Page

In this lesson, you learn how to create or revise your personal Facebook Profile page in a way that makes it friendly to your business. You receive a quick tour of signing up for Facebook, finding Facebook friends, editing your profile, adding status updates, and changing your privacy settings.

What Makes a Personal Page Business-Friendly?

You might not have a personal page on Facebook yet. If not, this lesson will take you very quickly through the basics of setting up a personal Facebook Page—and in a way that's friendly to your business page.

Or you may already have a personal page but have not thought much about how it interacts with your business persona. If so, read through this lesson for tips on how to see your personal site through business eyes.

This lesson is written for "principals"—people who are strongly associated with their business' web presence, such as a shop owner, marketing manager, principal in a consulting practice, and so on. For people who are employees of a business but aren't strongly associated with its management, the need to have your personal Facebook Page be business-friendly is not as strong.

Another big part of having a successful business Facebook presence is having some warmth and personality. So the point of looking at your Facebook presence through a business lens is not to scrub it of all signs of a personal life. It's just to avoid posting the occasional risqué picture or poor choice of words that could truly reflect poorly on your business—or at least to direct such postings only to your personal friends and not to business colleagues and potential customers.

It's also important how you reflect on your work life on your personal Facebook Page. You'll want to watch complaining vociferously about "stupid customers," for instance, or bragging about how much money the business made from having a sale. Important eyes are on you.

> TIP: **Groups Can Help—Up to a Point**
> The good news is that Facebook Groups can help you manage who sees what. You can create groups for personal friends, family members, and so on and restrict specific postings and specific photos to specific groups. There are two pieces of bad news, though: This is a hassle, and it's easy to slip up. Also it's easy for someone to copy a comment from any Group into an email or a Facebook comment of their own and share it. So while Groups offer some protection for banter and general snarkiness, you still need to avoid being obscene, slanderous, or discussing anything illegal—or anything else that could seriously hurt your business.

So you do need to think about what you're saying and potentially hold back a bit. It's also problematic, though, to become too bland and self-promoting. This is a general problem with Facebook, even strictly on the personal side: People mostly exchange pleasantries and good news to avoid hurt feelings or some kind of problem down the road. I guess that's what the phone and meeting up in person are for.

As a businessperson, you want to be seen as a "pillar of your community." For a local business, that's the community in which you live; for an online business, it might be a community of people who share certain interests and therefore buy your products. In any event, as a businessperson, you hold a position of trust, so what you say online can deeply affect others and potentially hurt that very position.

A good guideline is to post about your own feelings, rather than criticism of someone else. It would generally be OK to say you were frustrated by some incident at work or happy about how a promotion went. But perhaps it wouldn't be best to say what a jerk someone was or just how big your profit margins have become. So talk about your own feelings—without hurting anyone else's.

> CAUTION: **Don't Tread on Employees' Freedom**
> It's easy to be heavy-handed about the personal Facebook presence of employees, which is likely to be very important to them. Use a light touch in asking employees to change anything. If you do feel the need to request changes, try to restrict the changes to content that's publicly visible so people can "speak freely" with their Facebook friends. They will still have to be careful, though, about naming (or giving too much detail about) any individual they have a hard time with or dislike intensely, even with their best Facebook friends.

Creating a Business-Only "Personal" Page

A Facebook Profile page "belongs" to a specific individual's Facebook account. And you can't create a separate account for business use; Facebook's terms of service say an individual can only have one account.

When you create a fan page, it's tied to your personal account. You can create several fan pages—and they don't all have to be about you or your business. You can create a fan page for Elvis Presley, for instance, if you'd like; it certainly won't be the first, or the last, one on Facebook.

If you want to keep the Facebook Page separate from your (or anyone else's) actual personal account, create a new "personal" Facebook account—using the instructions in this lesson—that's designed only for "holding" one or more Facebook Pages related to business. You'll have to use this as your actual personal account as well, and delete any previous Facebook account that you had.

To do so, begin by creating an email address just for this purpose. For convenience and flexibility, use a webmail service such as Gmail, Yahoo! Mail, or Microsoft Hotmail. (Gmail is the most flexible of the three for the purposes described here.) Create a username and use a password that you're happy to share among the people who will be accessing the Facebook Page associated with this Facebook account.

Now when you create a new "personal" Facebook Page, you'll use the new email address that you just created and a password that you're happy sharing among several people.

Finally, set up this Facebook Page for your business using the instructions in this book. It will be more flexible because it's not tied to anyone's personal Facebook account.

Signing Up for Facebook

You begin your Facebook adventure by signing up. In the online world, it seems, half of life is signing up—rather than showing up, as Woody Allen once joked.

Signing up for Facebook is simple. The sign-up screen, showing everything you need to enter, is shown in Figure 2.1.

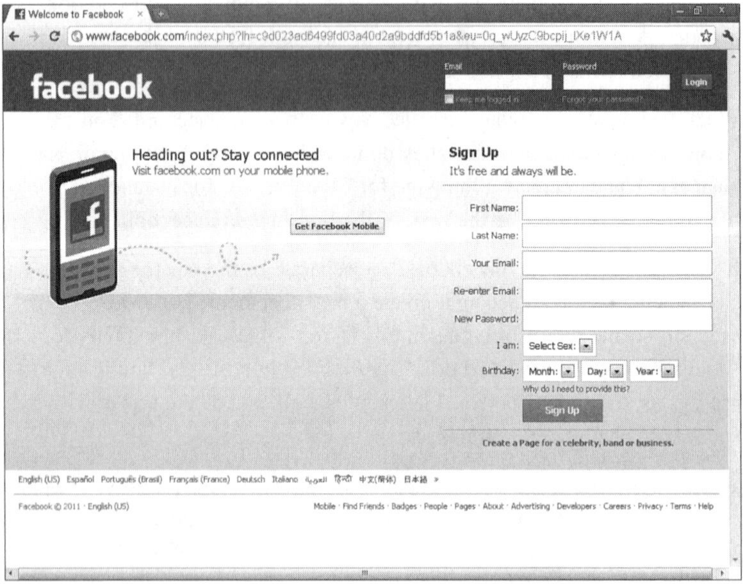

FIGURE 2.1   Signing up for Facebook is easy.

A few comments about the information you enter where there are business-relevant considerations are

▶ **First Name and Last Name.** Use your "official" name; for instance, I use Floyd Earl Smith, as on my birth certificate, even though my nickname and pen name is Bud E. Smith.

▶ **Your Email.** Be sure to use an email address that you'll always have access to. For instance, if you use a work email address and quit or lose your job, you could lose access to your Facebook account. The same thing can happen with an address provided by a mobile phone company or similar. This can cause you huge problems with both your personal Facebook presence and with the fan page for your business.

TIP: **Consider Using "Cloud" Email**

It's a bit risky to have your personal Facebook account tied to an email address that's dependent on a potentially temporary business relationship, such as a job or a mobile phone contract. So consider using or creating a truly personal email account that you fully control, such as a Gmail account. That way, you don't risk losing this connection. (Facebook is notably poor at helping customers who lose access to their accounts in this kind of manner.) Leave the sign-on details with a couple of people you trust in case you fall ill, or in case you are, in the inelegant phrase often used in business continuity planning, "hit by a truck."

▶ **Password.** Be sure to use a relatively safe and secure password, not something easy like "passw0rd." You won't want someone guessing your password, then posting under your name and potentially causing you—and your business—problems.

▶ **Birthday.** Enter this accurately for verification purposes. However, don't show your full birthday (that is, your birthday including the year) on Facebook—that makes things too easy for identity thieves.

When you click the Sign Up button, the account is created. Congratulations—you're on Facebook!

Finding Friends

Facebook makes it easy to tell people that you're on board. They encourage you to email all the people in your address book, asking them to become your friends on Facebook.

You can also find friends by searching for them within Facebook. However, unless a friend has a fairly distinctive name, you might have a difficult time finding her this way. She might also have set her security preferences so she can't be found through search. You could just ask her to "friend" you instead, if you're the one with the more distinctive name or the less extensive security protection. Or you can simply find each other through mutual friends who are on Facebook.

After you've "friended" the people you want to, though, you might not see all of them that often on Facebook. That's because, over time, Facebook will only show updates from a certain number of people in the Top News part of your Facebook News Feed. (Top News is the default.) My own News Feed is shown in Figure 2.2. Note how there's only room for one or two updates in each screen of Facebook content.

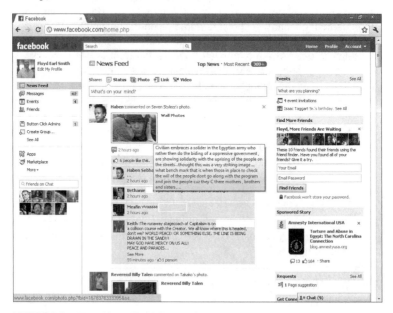

FIGURE 2.2   Your News Feed fills up fast.

You don't want to spend your time looking through updates of people you barely know, and you don't want updates from prolific Facebook users who you don't know very well to crowd out those from your true friends, close family members, and business colleagues. So I suggest that you be very selective at first as to whom you make friends with.

Over time, you'll probably end up with too many Facebook friends anyway, as we all tend to casually offer and accept Facebook friend requests. But there's no sense in starting out with too many Facebook friends on day one. Be selective with whom you invite.

The same is true, ironically, of Facebook fan pages that you "Like." Updates from pages that you "follow" can also fill up your News Feed. Currently, Facebook has a limit of 500 "Likes" per user, but you may well never reach that limit yourself.

Because you'll want people to "Like" your page, pay close attention to what you do appreciate, and what you don't appreciate, from the pages that you "Like" yourself.

Editing Your Profile

Entering and editing the information in your profile is really important. The old saying is, "You only get one chance to make a first impression." Your Facebook profile gives a strong first impression of you. And because you automatically go to your News Feed each day, it's easy for you to ignore your Profile.

At the beginning of 2011, Facebook updated Profiles to include a strip of personal information and photos across the top. The strip of personal information and photos for my own Profile is shown in Figure 2.3.

FIGURE 2.3   Your Profile includes random photos and data from your Info.

A long-time friend recently uploaded a bunch of photos of me with an old girlfriend, so that's what's up there now! As you can see from this example, it's easy for your Profile to give the wrong impression.

Facebook also makes available an Info page that's the source for the information across the top of your Profile. My Info page is shown in Figure 2.4. Note how, just like the News Feed, there's not that much information per screen; you have to scroll down quite a bit to get the whole picture.

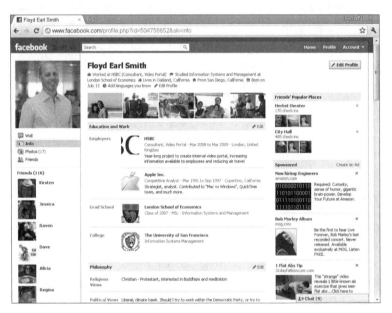

FIGURE 2.4   Your Info page shows highlights from your Profile.

To change the information shown in your Profile, simply click the link in the upper-right corner, Edit Profile, shown in Figure 2.4. A few things to keep in mind about your Profile include:

▶ **Keep it short and simple (KISS).** There's no need to list every employer you've ever had—that's what LinkedIn is for. (LinkedIn is a popular service for tracking your career and hosting your resume.) Just list the most meaningful ones that you feel most attached to. If you have too many, delete some.

▶ **Hit the Save Changes button a lot.** As you edit your information, it's easy to surf away without saving your changes and lose them. Hit the Save Changes button frequently as you work.

▶ **Use a good profile picture.** I often don't photograph well, and the profile picture I use was taken by a professional photographer a couple of years ago at work. However, it's also good to change your picture occasionally, so look for fresh photos that show you in a good light where you can.

▶ **Fill in your Philosophy.** Your Philosophy, shown in Figure 2.5, is one of the few areas here where you really get to be creative and personal. This is where you describe your religion, political views, people who inspire you, and favorite quotations. Give this careful thought and update it frequently.

FIGURE 2.5   Getting your Philosophy right is important.

▶ **Edit Arts & Entertainment, Sports, Activities and Interests.** These areas are filled in by what you "Like" and by explicit choices you make. Only the first few entries are displayed on your Profile, but you can drag and drop to move new things to the top.

▶ **Contact information.** You can fill in your address, phone number, mobile phone number, and so on. This might sometimes be useful for friends trying to reach you or for prefilling in information if you buy something through Facebook. However, getting access to this kind of information is an identity thief or email spammer's dream. So I recommend that you don't enter contact information at all; you can't accidentally expose it to the wrong people if you never enter it into Facebook.

CAUTION: **Don't Enter Your Address or Phone Number into Your Profile**

In January 2011, Facebook announced that they would include your address and phone number in the information you reveal when an application asks if it can access your profile. Angry comments from users followed, noting that people often allow profile access without really looking at the fine print or thinking through the details. Facebook changed its plans—for now. The point remains that if you never enter certain information into Facebook, Facebook can't share it with the wrong people.

Changing Privacy Settings

Privacy is hugely controversial on Facebook. It's worth understanding the background a little bit.

We live in a world where an amazing amount of anonymity is possible. People can be into all sorts of interesting and unusual things without very many people in their lives knowing about it. Friends, work, and family can be in totally different spheres.

Until Facebook. With Facebook, these different realms are brought together. Family members can see that you were "tagged" in a photo taken at a strip club; friends can see that you're spending the holidays with the old boyfriend or girlfriend that you never told them about. Importantly, your boss can see your check-in at the airport when you said you were home sick. Or, a friend can check you in at a bar without your even knowing about it. (And, perhaps, without you actually being there.) This kind of cross-talk can cause anything from mild embarrassment to losing friends, losing a job, or divorce.

There are a couple of ways to guard against this. One is to watch what you do and who you do it with. Another is to try to manage the flow of information about what you do. This can partly be accomplished by staying out of potentially embarrassing photos, asking friends not to mention some of your whereabouts on Facebook, and so on. Another is through managing your Facebook privacy settings.

CAUTION: **Facebook Changes Privacy Settings Often**

Facebook has made many changes to their privacy settings over the years. Mark Zuckerberg, Facebook founder and CEO, says people should just expect less privacy in this digital age—and Facebook has played a big part in making this happen, for better or worse. At the same time, Facebook sometimes reacts to complaints by adding new privacy tools. The result, intended or not, is that it's very hard to get your privacy settings right and to stay on top of them through all the changes. Even staying off Facebook doesn't help; you can still get tagged in a photo, checked in someplace, or mentioned in a status update that goes out to people who you didn't want to share your location or activities with.

Your Facebook privacy settings are complicated, and the settings available change frequently, so trying to stop news from travelling by using them is never likely to be 100% effective. It's worth a try, though, and might prevent some hassle or embarrassment at some point.

You can put your Facebook friends into Groups, such as Family, Friends, and Work. Then you can have status updates only go out to one or more groups and exclude others.

I don't really recommend this, though, for business use partly because it's complicated and easy to mess up and can lead you into difficulties. Also for business purposes, you want your status updates to reach as wide an audience as possible—simply to keep people up to date and interested in your activities, personal and professional.

If you're really dedicated to spending the time and effort to manage groups and to still keep a reasonable number of status updates going out to a broad audience as well as to narrow ones, by all means, go ahead. But for most of us, it's less trouble to simply manage what we say on Facebook. (And to manage what we do in life so that others don't have too much embarrassing material about us to post on Facebook.)

The other privacy setting of concern to business, though, is one that I do recommend—but not for you, the owner or manager of a business. This is the ability to hide as much as you want of your profile information from your publicly available Facebook Page. This means restricting your Facebook profile to just your Facebook friends.

In most cases, as the principal of a business, you don't want this. You want to be discoverable on Facebook to the general public via Google, through Facebook, and so on. You want people who aren't your Facebook friends to still be able to see what you're up to.

However, your employees are a different matter. If their activities are potentially embarrassing to the business, I don't think it's unreasonable to ask them to restrict the visibility of their Facebook Walls or Profile pages to just their Facebook friends. This is not perfect protection, but it does represent a solid effort to help separate work and personal spheres.

Of course, you might wish to do this yourself, for your own Profile page, as well. It's a big deal to have your Facebook updates available to the world at large. So you may want to have this level of privacy protection, even if it reduces the visibility of your business a little bit by reducing the visibility of, well, you.

To hide a fair amount or all your Facebook information from people who aren't your Facebook friends, follow these steps:

1. Sign into Facebook and click **Edit My Profile** in the upper-left corner of the screen.

   Your profile information then appears.

2. Click the **Privacy settings** link in the left corner. (You can also go directly to these settings from any page by clicking Privacy

Settings from the Account drop-down link at the upper-right corner of the screen.)

Now your privacy settings appear.

3. Click the **Customize settings** link.

Detailed settings appear, as shown in Figure 2.6.

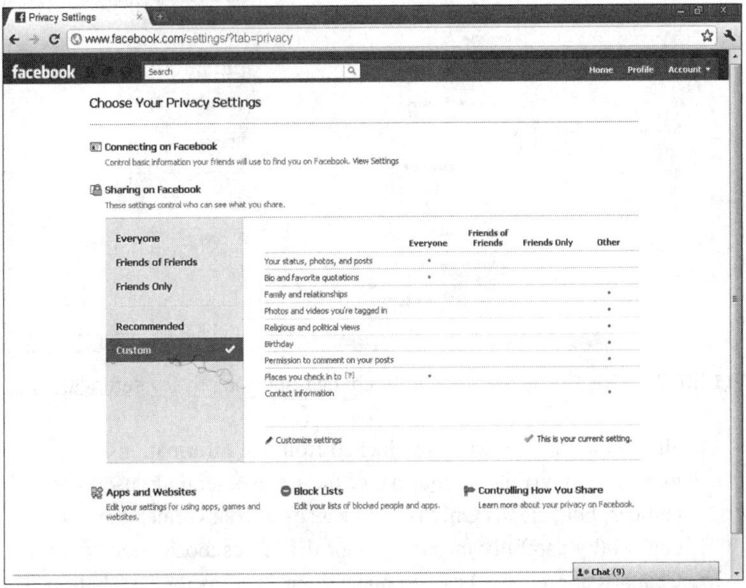

FIGURE 2.6 Facebook privacy settings are complicated but ultimately manageable.

4. Click the **Customize settings** link in the lower-middle portion of the screen.

Pull-down menus appear for your privacy settings, as shown in Figure 2.7.

5. Change most or all the settings to only your Facebook friends by using the pull-down menus and clicking **Friends Only**.

The choices are Everyone; Friends of Friends; Friends Only; and Customize, which allows you to choose specific people to be

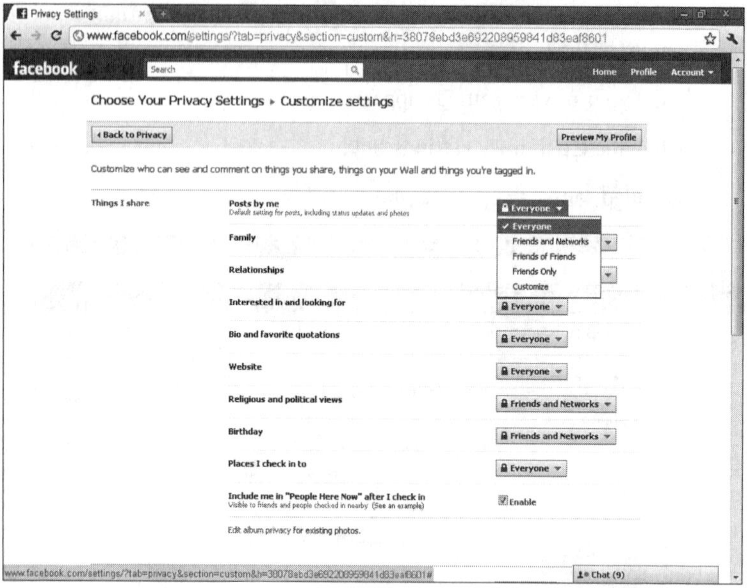

FIGURE 2.7   Use pull-down menus to change specific privacy settings.

allowed to view or who are blocked from the information—or make it only visible to you. All of these are potentially useful choices, but Friends Only is the easiest setting to remember and control (by carefully managing your list of Facebook friends). Changes are recorded as you make them; there is no Save button.

6. To see how your page looks to visitors, click the **Preview My Profile** button. A preview of your profile appears.

7. To see how your page looks to specific people, enter a person's name.

8. Click the **Back to Privacy** button to return to the screen shown in Figure 2.6.

9. Repeat steps 4–7 until you're happy with the results. When you're done, navigate back to your News Feed page via the **Home** link at the top of the page or to your Profile page by clicking the Profile link.

You can manage your own privacy settings in this way, but you can also use these steps to help your employees do the same. You can even have them log in, open up the privacy area, and help them make the changes right in their Facebook accounts. Changing the settings to Friends Only means that the experience of the specific user and their friends is unchanged; it's only people outside the friends circle who see less information.

> **NOTE: Most Facebook Apps Not Covered Here**
>
> Facebook Apps are an important part of your Facebook experience, but the apps you put on your personal Facebook Page have little to no impact on your business use of your page. Therefore I only cover apps briefly, in Lesson 3, "Finding and Installing Apps." For information about using apps in your personal Facebook Page, see *Sams Teach Yourself Facebook in 10 Minutes.*

Sharing Your Status

Facebook is supposed to be all about entering and updating your status. That's how people know what you're up to, how you're responding to the events of the day, and so on. Entering status updates also provides you with a surprisingly valuable and meaningful record of your own life, one small entry at a time. A few status updates on a Profile page are shown in Figure 2.8.

"Checking in" in Facebook Places, as described in the next lesson, is just a particular kind of status update.

With all you have to manage in your life day in and day out, it's surprisingly easy to forget to enter your status very often or to even check in. As you look at your News Feed each day, or if you're like me, many times each day, it's easy to light up on seeing a friend's comment, enter a response, even plan to attend an event, and feel like you're plugged in. But you're only partly plugged in if you're not updating your own status.

So the main "to do" for having a business-friendly Facebook personal page is simply to share your status and check in using Facebook Places—a lot. Enter status updates and check in as often as makes sense—and then a bit more. This is the main way your Facebook friends really get to know you.

FIGURE 2.8   Entering status updates is the heart of your Facebook presence.

Here are a few quick tips for getting the most out of each type of status update plus check-ins:

▶ **Status.** This is a brief entry, up to 460 characters, prompted by the question in the entry box: "What's on your mind?" Just answer the question. Try to do this kind of update at least once a day, to keep your Facebook presence fresh. For business purposes, don't be too obscure or disturbing; not everyone who sees your updates will know your quirky sense of humor if you have one. But do share.

▶ **Photos.** Take lots of photos. Post the best of them. Tag people in them. (Most people love this, and it's great for building connections with friends and groups.) For business purposes, just take

and post business-related photos in the same way that you do
personal photos: frequently. Be a bit careful with the content and
don't embarrass anyone very much, including yourself.

> TIP: **Take Care with Photos**
> With photos of other people or mentions of them, leaving them feel-
> ing a bit chagrined is okay; truly embarrassed, not so much.
> Catching your friend sitting at a bar with a shot and a beer in front
> of them is probably all right, with permission; catching them making
> goo-goo eyes at a person who is not their significant other is a defi-
> nite no-no. (Go ahead and take the picture, and share it with your
> friend; just don't put it on Facebook.)

▶ **Links.** I use this a lot. As you're Web-surfing, capture the URLs
  of pages you like—articles, events, fund-raisers, and so on. Then
  paste the URL into a Link update on Facebook. You can add a
  comment, but don't go all *War and Peace* about it—just indicate
  your opinion briefly, and point out if you're calling on anyone to
  do something or asking for feedback. For business, avoid the
  most controversial links and anything indecent, but definitely do
  include some links related to your work and your interests.

▶ **Videos.** I don't use this much because I don't have the patience
  to watch much Web video. But many people love Web video and
  use video updates to great effect. For videos you take yourself,
  the rules are the same as for photos—don't embarrass anyone;
  nothing too controversial or indecent; and, be sure to include
  videos related to your area of business.

▶ **Checking in to Places.** You really want to encourage others to
  check in to your Facebook Places page if you have a physical
  place of business, so check in to all sorts of places as you go
  through your day, as described in the next lesson. Of course that
  doesn't include strip clubs (even as a joke) or even too many
  check-ins to regular bars. Again, you're a pillar of the community; show that you frequent (reputable) establishments all over
  your stomping grounds.

In addition to making status updates, much of your personal Facebook time will be spent "liking" and commenting on updates that other people enter. These responses go back to the person who entered the original comment and their Facebook friends, unless someone fine-tunes their privacy settings to restrict this. This can be a lot of fun, but it can also be embarrassing. For example, if one of your Facebook friends makes a mildly snarky comment about your old boss, and you are even more snarky in return—and your Facebook friend happens to be your old boss's Facebook friend, the boss will see your comment.

More on the personal side, let's say your old flame is still your Facebook friend. You may be subjected to an endless stream of photos, comments, notices that they both "like" something, and other affectionate ephemera between them. Not always a lot of fun!

People usually have a learning curve and make embarrassing or even painful mistakes in any new medium. These are sometimes related in jokes and stories about errant telephone calls, answering machine messages, email messages, and more. Facebook is just another new way to enjoy—and potentially embarrass—yourself. Let the user beware.

> NOTE: **Adding Apps to Your Facebook Page**
>
> Using the App Directory and adding apps to your Facebook Page is described in Lesson 4, "Choosing Your Facebook Business Strategy."

Summary

In this lesson, you learned how to create or revise your personal Facebook Profile page in a business-friendly manner. You took a quick tour of signing up for Facebook, finding Facebook friends, editing your profile, adding status updates, and changing your privacy settings. In the next lesson, you learn how to find and install apps, on either your personal Profile or your Facebook fan page.

LESSON 3
Finding and Installing Apps

In this lesson, you learn how to find and install apps for your Facebook presence, both for your personal Profile page and the fan page for your business. You learn different methods of searching for apps and information about them, including a detailed description of how to use the Facebook App Directory.

Choosing Apps for Business and Pleasure

Facebook has literally thousands of apps you can add to your personal Profile and the fan page for your business. You can use Facebook apps to play games, bring in information, or give your fan page visitors something to do.

You're likely to want to put some apps on your personal Profile just for your own use. In addition, I suggest that you use your personal Profile as a kind of staging ground and test area for business-oriented apps and then put the ones that prove worthwhile on the fan page for your business. This gives you a chance to really separate the wheat from the chaff, and to keep apps that don't work well (or that do funny things with people's information, like giving it to email spammers) off your business page.

> NOTE: **Installing Apps to Different Pages**
> This lesson shows you how to find apps for either your personal Profile page or your business fan page. It also shows you how to install apps on your personal Profile page. Installing apps on your business fan page is a bit different and is covered in Lesson 7, "Setting Up Your Business Fan Page."

Finding apps is a bit of a pain because there are so many of them. In this way, Facebook's Apps Directory is like Apple's App Store for the iPhone and iPad, Android Market for Android phones, and other popular application clearinghouses. The very popularity of apps makes it hard to find the ones you really need.

Setting up apps can be anything from easy to quite difficult. Some apps need a lot of configuration to set up their look and feel and to get information from various places on the Internet; others are plug and play.

When you explore the Facebook Apps Directory, you see that it highlights popular and recently added apps. Here are some ways to keep up with apps that may be suitable for your Facebook Pages:

▶ **Check the Apps Directory regularly.** The New area is updated regularly, and the Most Popular area changes over time, too. The Business category provides a home for apps most likely to be suitable for your fan page. So check back frequently, perhaps once a week.

▶ **Keep an eye on other Facebook Pages.** As you use Facebook, look for promising apps on others' pages—especially the fan page of other businesses. When you see an app you like, make a note of it; otherwise, it's too easy to forget how to find it again.

▶ **Look for articles with recommendations.** Many online sites track Facebook. A Google search for "top Facebook business apps," for instance, helps you find sites worth bookmarking. Two of my favorite sites for Facebook app information are Mashable, at www.mashable.com, and eHow, at www.ehow.com. Figure 3.1 shows one of the helpful articles on eHow.

▶ **Ask friends and colleagues.** Many Facebook users are quite familiar with apps they like—and apps they don't. You can get great recommendations from others.

▶ **Imagine what you'd like and search for it.** If you're running a local sporting goods store, and there's a surge of interest in cycling, you might want to add an app with the latest cycling news and information. Search for it in the Apps Directory; there's a good chance you'll find something useful there.

FIGURE 3.1   eHow covers Facebook and much more.

CAUTION: **Check Your Apps Carefully**

Some Facebook apps have undesirable aspects to them; they ask for too much information from users, for instance, and then sell it on to others who may use it to send spam. Even a formerly trust-worthy and useful app can suddenly change into a bad actor. So be careful which apps you add and keep an eye on them; if the apps that you put on your personal Profile page or your business fan page act badly, it reflects badly on you.

Looking for Facebook Apps

Looking for Facebook Apps is kind of fun *and* kind of a pain. But keeping up with the latest and greatest, especially in your industry, is important for your personal Facebook presence and for your business presence as well.

People don't necessarily expect your business to have the world's whizzi-est fan page. They do expect you, though, to know what's going on in your field. If you run a wine shop, and there's a cool app for choosing wine to go with food, you'll earn brownie points if you find it, make it available on your fan page, and let people know it's there.

So staying on top of what's new in apps isn't a technical exercise; it's part of extending your core expertise around your business.

Follow these steps to check the Apps Directory:

1. Open your personal Profile page to your Wall (the Home tab) or your Profile.

2. Click the **Apps** link in the left-hand rail.

   The Apps page opens, as shown in Figure 3.2, showing apps that you and your Facebook friends use.

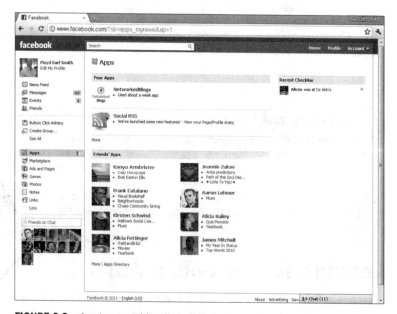

FIGURE 3.2   I get apps with a little help from my friends.

3. Click the **Apps Directory** link at the bottom of the page.

The Apps Directory opens, as shown in Figure 3.3. The All Apps category is selected in the navigation on the left. The area at the top, Featured by Facebook, is likely to include apps promoted by Facebook in return for a payment or some other consideration. The Apps You May Like area in the middle has apps that have been chosen based on your Facebook usage.

FIGURE 3.3 The Apps Directory makes recommendations for you.

These two areas stay the same when you click on a particular category, as described in the next step. The bottom area, when you first come onto the page, is Recent Activity from Friends, and it shows activity from all across the Web by your Facebook friends. When you choose a category in the left-hand navigation, the bottom area changes, though, to show specific apps.

4. Click a category name, such as **Business**.

The lower area of the page changes to show specific apps in the category you chose, as shown in Figure 3.4. Note the controls on the page carefully, as they'll help you find what you need. There's an **All Business** pull-down menu in the upper right showing subcategories within Business—Finance, General, and Other, at this writing. In the Business area, there are two separate categories: Popular and Recently Added.

FIGURE 3.4   The Apps Directory is your gateway to thousands of apps.

5. Try the pull-down menu in the upper right to hone in on subcategories. For Business, try **All Business** (the default), **Finance**, **General**, and **Other**.

The apps change to reflect the category you choose.

6. Click the **Popular** and **Recently Added** buttons to see the highlighted apps of each type.

If an app looks interesting, read the description—example shown in Figure 3.5. Note the number of active users, the number of your Facebook friends who use the app, and the star rating for the app, based on user feedback.

Star Rating

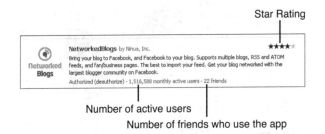

Number of active users
Number of friends who use the app

FIGURE 3.5   Brief descriptions tell you a lot about apps.

7. To see a detailed description of an app, click the app's name or logo.

A detailed description appears, as shown in Figure 3.6. Note that the description is a fan page, which is what you're going to create for your business as well. Note the number of reviews, shown on the left side; click to see the reviews themselves. Note the number of your Facebook friends who use the app and click to see who they are.

After you've finished installing the app, the Remove App link appears here. Return to this page if you need to remove the app later.

TIP: **Give Networked Blogs a Try**

The app shown in the figures, NetworkedBlogs, is a popular app for business. If you have a blog or are thinking of starting one, consider using this app to integrate it into Facebook.

FIGURE 3.6 Each app has its own Facebook Page.

8. To get updates about the app in your News Feed, click the **Like** button.

   Information posted by the app's creators will appear on your News Feed in Facebook. This is also a good way to be reminded about an app if you're not sure whether you want to download it right now.

9. To install the app, click the **Go to App** button.

   A request for permission appears, as shown in Figure 3.7.

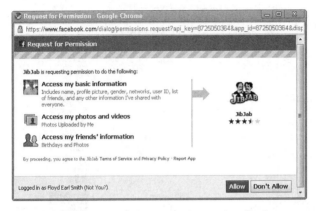

FIGURE 3.7   Look carefully to see what you're allowing.

CAUTION: Look Carefully at Permissions

Look carefully at what permissions you're granting when you add an app to either your personal page or your fan page. For instance, if an app is about gambling and requests permission to post to your Wall, you might not like the tone and volume of gambling information that you then end up seeing. But if the app asks for permission to post status updates from you, it's your Facebook friends who may learn more about your interests than you were looking to share.

---

10. To proceed, click **Allow**.

A page of settings might appear, as shown in Figure 3.8.

11. Fill in the settings for the app.

12. The app will now appear in your Apps list and will "do what it says on the tin"—such as sending you daily news updates, making a shared calendar available to you and your friends, and so on.

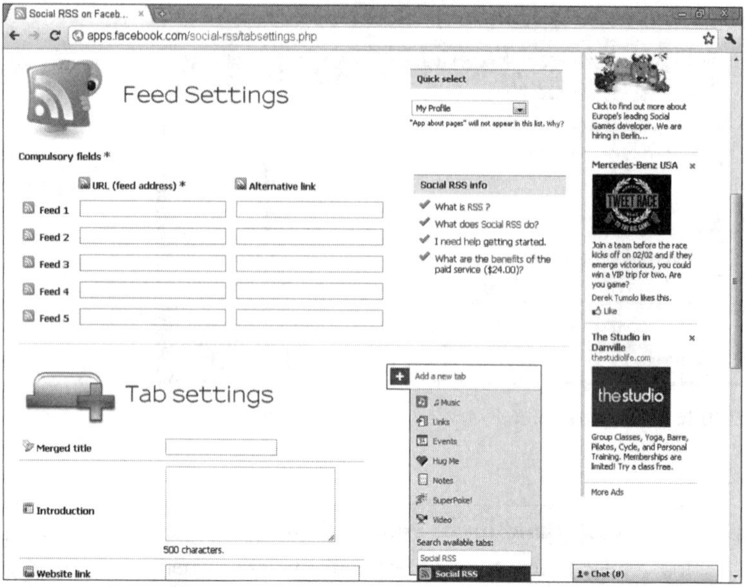

FIGURE 3.8   The app you're checking out might or might not have many settings.

Summary

In this lesson you learned how to find and install apps for your Facebook presence, both for your personal Profile page and the fan page for your business. You learned different methods of searching for apps and information about them, including a detailed description of how to use the Facebook App Directory. In the next lesson, you learn how to choose your Facebook business strategy.

LESSON 4

Choosing Your Facebook Business Strategy

In this lesson, you learn how to create a Facebook-first online strategy for your business. You learn how Facebook Pages (also known as "fan pages"), Places pages, Facebook Deals, and Facebook Ads work together. You also learn how to "check in" to a Place on Facebook, and get tips for pulling all the pieces together.

Leading with Facebook First

Marketing simply means "the things you do to help support selling." It includes advertising, pricing, offering deals, presenting your goods and services for sale, and more. Even small details of the way you interact with people are part of your marketing.

Marketing is part of everything you do in business. It's even part of everything you do in nonprofit or government organizations, where "closing the sale" might not involve making money; it mean helping someone or preventing wrongdoing.

Facebook will never be your whole marketing strategy—but it can be a great place to start or a way to promote a strategy you already have in place. It's a kind of online sandbox through which you can communicate with part of your customer (or client) base in a controlled manner and measure the results.

You can accomplish a lot for your business through Facebook and use what you learn to improve your marketing in the rest of your business as well.

So Facebook is just part of your overall marketing approach, with its own strengths and weaknesses. What should you keep in mind as you get into marketing with Facebook? Here are half a dozen "rules of the road":

- ▶ **Half of life is showing up.** For some audiences, there's nothing worse than for a business they want to patronize to not be on Facebook. If college-educated people under 30 are part of your customer base—as they probably are—then you have to wade in and develop a Facebook presence. You'll make mistakes; you might waste some money, and you'll certainly waste some time. But you'll end up way ahead of those who don't get involved.

- ▶ **Try everything (at least) once.** Resolve to set up a fan page for your business. Make regular status updates and respond to others. Also set up a Places page. Then offer Deals and try creating and running at least a couple of Facebook Ads. By doing this, all these tools become part of your repertoire—there for you to deploy right away, or whenever you're ready.

- ▶ **Know who you are.** Businesses usually can be classed as lowest price, best product/service, or best (customer) service. Which are you? How do you present that in a positive way within the uniform, blue and white Facebook interface? Within your Facebook presence, emphasize what it is that makes your business special. Figure 4.1 shows the Facebook presence of Pep Boys, a business famous for low prices, but which also cultivates a sense of fun around their business and offerings.

- ▶ **Know what you want to accomplish.** Know what you're trying to accomplish with each post you make on Facebook, each Facebook Ad, each Facebook Deal. Even a seemingly vague purpose, like posting so that you "engage better with this group of customers," will help guide you. A more specific purpose, like "to sell the rest of the mauve bicycle helmets," is measurable and actionable.

- ▶ **Say little—well.** Make fewer posts than you might want to, but make them well-written and, please, edit carefully. A casual approach to spelling and punctuation is okay among Facebook friends but not for you as the person representing your business.

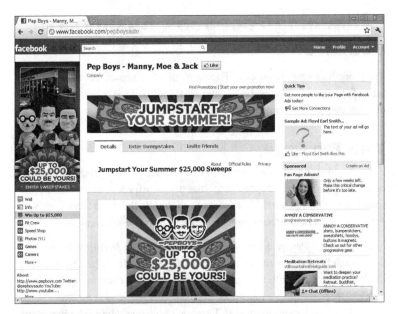

FIGURE 4.1 Pep Boys is friendly on Facebook.

(Yes, this goes for your personal page as well as for your business presence.)

▶ **Measure your inputs and outputs.** When you get your Facebook presence set up, keep track of how much time you spend on Facebook and of the results you achieve. This will help you "right-size" your efforts so you get the most bang for your buck on Facebook.

If you use these rules to guide what you do in Facebook, you'll find that your work and accomplishments—which you'll have written down and measured, of course—can be easily extended to other marketing efforts, online and offline.

Also because Facebook is growing so fast, it's often the prism through which opinion-formers view the whole online world. You're likely to find that your Facebook marketing efforts give you and your business a certain cachet that you can't gain any other way.

Examining Facebook Business Features

There are four main features of Facebook that businesses can take advantage of: fan pages, Places, Deals, and Ads. Following is a brief summary of what they are and how they work together.

Your Fan Page

Every business of any size should have a fan page. This is the "home base" for your Facebook presence, what people expect to see when they search for your business. Your fan page should be linked to from Facebook Ads, your Facebook Places page, and often by Facebook Deals as well.

Your Facebook Page is like a simple website for your business. If you don't already have a website, a Facebook Page is a great place to start on the Web. This is mainly because the design work is easier, navigation is handled through tabs that are easy to create, and the look is already defined for you—everything is in Facebook blue and white. The Pep Boys Facebook Page in Figure 4.1 is a good example. Note how the logo has been modified to include a request to participate in a sweepstakes. I show you how to create a Facebook Page for your business in the next lesson.

Your Facebook Page doesn't cost you anything to create and maintain, just time and effort. You can usually create and manage it yourself or have a member of your staff do it if you're lucky enough to have a suitable person working for you. You can promote the Facebook Page for your business via an occasional mention on your personal Facebook Page as well.

The ability to easily manage the Facebook Page for your business yourself is a welcome change from websites, which usually cost money to set up and run—or look ugly and work poorly if done in-house. Figure 4.2 shows a website done by talented amateurs for Business and Technical Communications Services (BATCS), a UK-based company. You can visit the site at www.batcs.co.uk. As you'll see if you visit, it gets the job done but is a bit rough around the edges.

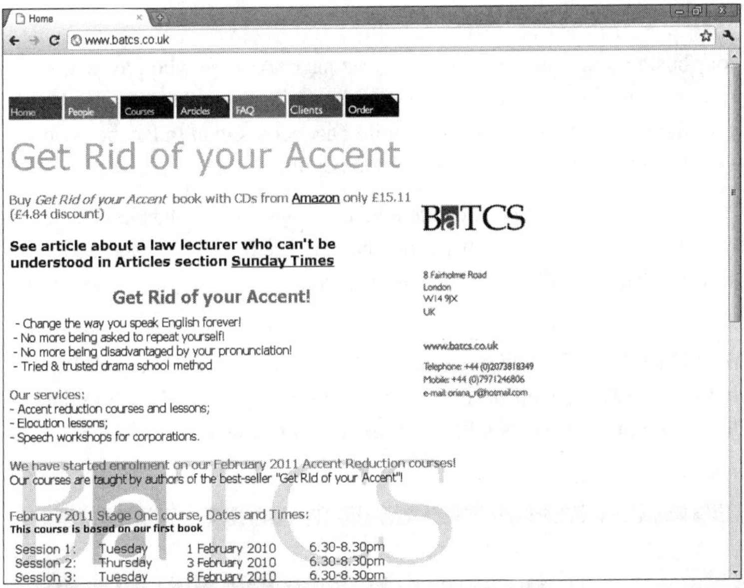

FIGURE 4.2   BATCS has a "rough and ready" website.

If you already have a website, your Facebook Page may well be more limited than your site. If this is true for you, you'll probably handle easy stuff on it; for instance, you might post on Facebook about new, hot deals. Then you direct viewers to your website for more information, e-commerce and so on.

In addition to your business' Facebook Page, you should also have a Places page, which is tied to your geographic location and hosts Deals. You'll get advice from Facebook and others to link your Facebook Page and your Places page.

I suggest you keep these separate. Each page can meet different needs. Big businesses keep their Facebook Pages and their Places pages separate; if you merge yours, you're basically telling the world, "I don't have a big business."

Your Places Page

Your business may already have a Places page. Anyone who physically visits your business or even comes near it can "check in" to your business from their mobile phones or the mobile Facebook site at m.facebook.com. (For the iPad, users go to touch.facebook.com.)

The person checking in can create a Places page for your business, and then check in to the Places page. So check to see if a Places page has already been created for your business. If not, you create your Places page yourself.

Your Places page is even more highly formatted than the Facebook Page that you create for your business. It's prefabricated—you just fill in the details. Figure 4.3 shows a Places page with a few details.

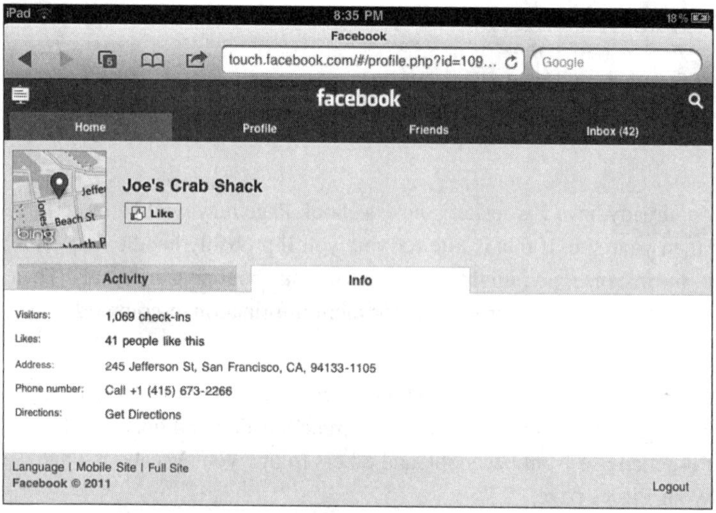

FIGURE 4.3　A Places page is easy to create.

Though boring to some, the consistency of Places pages is also reassuring to people who just want a "quick hit" of information about your business. Places pages are easy to create, easy to update, and easy to use.

Your Places page is free—like a free listing in the Yellow Pages—the only difference being that young people do use Facebook, and they don't use the Yellow Pages. It's one of the best deals around, and it's actually a bit silly that many businesses are not yet using it.

You can combine your Places page and your fan page into a single page, but I recommend keeping them separate. That way, your Places page is for people to use for checking in and for quick, urgent information such as your location, business hours, and phone number. Your Facebook Page is for more extensive information, for people to Like, and so on.

I describe how to create your Places page, or how to claim it if it already exists, in Lesson 9, "Claiming Your Places Page." I also describe how to combine it with your fan page, if you're so inclined.

Facebook Deals

It's easy to misunderstand the role of Facebook Deals. It sounds like a generic term—a business deal that you offer on Facebook. However, while you can definitely do that, a Facebook Deal (with a capital "D" in "Deal") is a specialized beast.

A Facebook Deal is only available to people who check in to a Facebook Place using, well, Facebook. This limited, exclusive approach, focused only on people who are physically in your business, makes visiting businesses like going on an Easter egg hunt.

But don't turn your customers into sad little children with empty plastic eggs; offer them Facebook Deals if you can. You can have an inexpensive, default Deal, such as a raffle entry or a small charitable donation with purchase, which you can use in between your bigger Deals.

Facebook Deals cost money to run; you pay Facebook to offer the deal, though Facebook offers free samples to get you started. You also have to pay the cost of the discount or other special offer that you put into the Deal, but you can do this in such a way that the Deal has a good chance of paying for itself in new business. For more information about costs and free samples, see Lesson 10, "Creating Facebook Deals."

An example of a Facebook Deal is shown in Figure 4.4. Your Deal can look quite similar—both in its "look and feel" and in its content—or quite different.

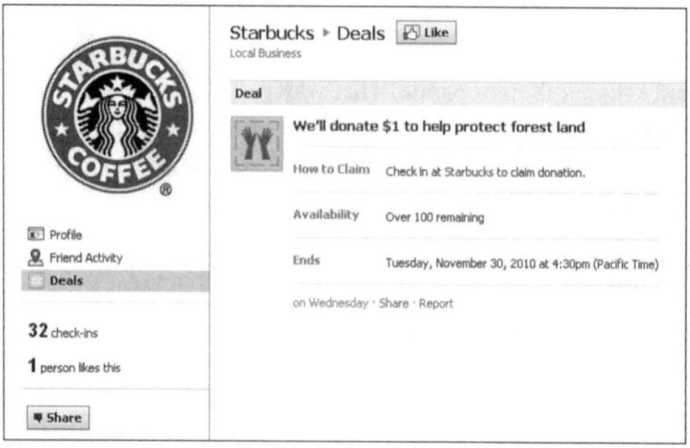

FIGURE 4.4   Consistently offer Deals to your customers.

The business sets up the Facebook Deal and chooses when to offer it. All the customer can do is come to the business, check in, and hope for a Deal. If customers try this several times and come up empty, they're likely to quit trying.

You can get them excited, though, by promoting Facebook Deals, featuring them in ads, putting up signage, and telling customers verbally about Deals that you're offering. My guess is that members of the main Facebook audience—young, mostly single, college-educated people who grew up on Facebook—will be quite excited about a Facebook Deal you offer.

So here's the lay of the land so far: In most cases, you'll have a Facebook Page and a Places page for your business, and you'll keep them separate. You'll then run Facebook Deals tied to your Places page. You'll promote your Facebook Deals on the Facebook Page for your business, as well as on your separate website (the nonFacebook one) and elsewhere.

Now where does this leave Facebook Ads? Well, Facebook Ads are a bit different than your Facebook Page, your Places Page, and Deals. They're distinct, potentially expensive, and a whole separate challenge.

Facebook Ads

Facebook Ads are very visible, and they're also the first thing most people will ask you about when you say you're doing business on Facebook. They're attention-getting and, so far, often seen as annoying and intrusive. Facebook advertising is relatively inexpensive but hard to get right, so it's largely done by people who are one step up from email scammers.

Facebook Ads are targeted by information in the user's profile. Perhaps unfortunately, the main targeting I've seen personally so far is by marital status. I'm just over 50, and when I first created my personal Facebook Page, I was single.

The column on the right side of my Profile page or News Feed—the "right-hand rail," in Web design parlance—was usually filled to overflowing with dating agency ads showing photos, which appeared to be digitally retouched, of attractive, buxom women who looked to be about ten years younger than I.

A bit later, I started dating someone and changed my status to "In a Relationship." The ads with the buxom ladies went away. There are many people who choose the null option (an empty relationship status) or "It's confusing," another favorite, just to avoid the age-targeted lonely hearts ads that otherwise show up in their Facebook Profile.

You have the opportunity to do better, though, with ads you create. By using Facebook's targeting options and your own detailed knowledge of your customers, you may well be able to create Facebook Ads that work well and that get you favorable attention from customers.

Facebook Ads definitely cost money to run. This is described in some detail in Lesson 12, "Pricing and Creating Your Ad Campaign." In that lesson, I introduce you to targeting options that can keep your costs down and your profits up.

Facebook Ads are not directly dependent on your Facebook Page, your Places page, or any Facebook Deals. However, just as it's a bit silly not to have a Places page (because it's free), it's also a bit silly to spend money on Facebook Ads without trying out the underlying offer and related ideas on your Facebook Page and/or Places page first. I suggest you get pretty good with the other elements before you sink very much money into Facebook Ads. You should definitely try Facebook Ads, however, early and often, after navigating the free aspects of Facebook.

Checking In to a Place

To set up your Facebook strategy, you need to understand the full range of experiencing the business side of Facebook. So far we've discussed Facebook Ads, which we all see when we use Facebook, as well as creating a fan page, creating a Places page, and what Facebook Deals are like. Now let's go through the process of checking in to a Place, to see what that's like for the user.

Checking in to a Place is a fun way of creating a status update. Facebook actually verifies that you're somewhere near the place in question before it lets you check in, and you can only use a mobile device or the mobile version of the Facebook site for check-ins. (There's no Places check-in capability on the full Facebook site, which, I admit, seems kind of odd.)

Instead of just answering the famous Facebook status update question, "What are you doing?" a Facebook Places check-in shows where you are, as well as giving you a chance to share your thoughts. A Places check-in also gives you the option to name the Facebook friends who are there with you, which makes it even more fun.

TIP: **Ask Friends Before You Check Them In**

Ask friends before you check them in. It's surprising how much embarrassment can be caused by sharing little details like where you were, exactly what time you were there, and just whom you were with.

Follow these steps to check in to a Facebook place:

1. On a mobile device, such as an iPhone or Android phone, go to the App Store (iPhone), the Android Market, or equivalent and search for "Facebook check-in" or similar. Find the free app and install it. On the iPad, go to touch.facebook.com. On a laptop, go to the Facebook mobile website at m.facebook.com.

The example shown in Figure 4.5 is the Facebook mobile website on the iPad. Your mileage may vary, depending on the device and app or version of the Facebook site you're using.

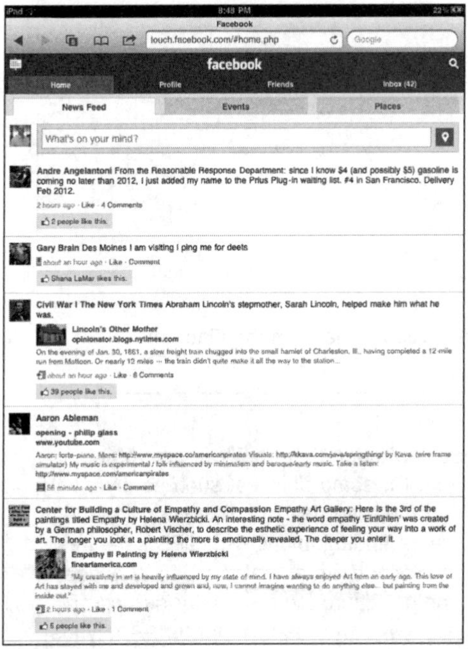

FIGURE 4.5 The iPad version of the Facebook site is mobile-ized.

2. Click the **Places** tab in the upper-right area of the screen.

   The Places area appears, as shown in Figure 4.6.

3. Click the **Share Where You Are With Friends** link.

   A list of places you've checked into in the past appears—if this is your first time checking in, the list will be empty.

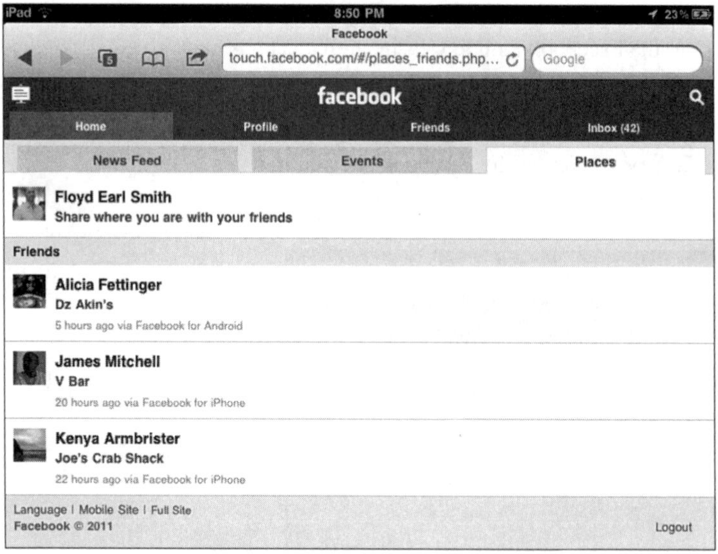

FIGURE 4.6   Checking in to a Facebook Place on the iPad.

TIP: **Getting a Location**

Facebook Places sometimes can't identify where you are, which prevents you from checking in. On some devices, such as my Android phone, it helps to turn on a setting that enables wireless networks to be used for location finding, along with GPS satellites. On Android in the Location & Security area, look for Use Wireless Networks and turn the setting on. There isn't a similar setting on the iPhone or iPad, but these devices do use the feature—they just don't let you turn it off.

---

4. Pick one of the places you've formerly been, if that's appropriate, or press the entry area next to the word Add. Start typing in the name of your location. If the place is listed, its name appears; press it. If the place isn't already listed, you'll see the words "No place matching 'xxx,'" and it's a new Place. Type the full name and press Add.

For a new Place, a map showing where you are appears, along with fields for the name and (optional) description, as shown in Figure 4.7.

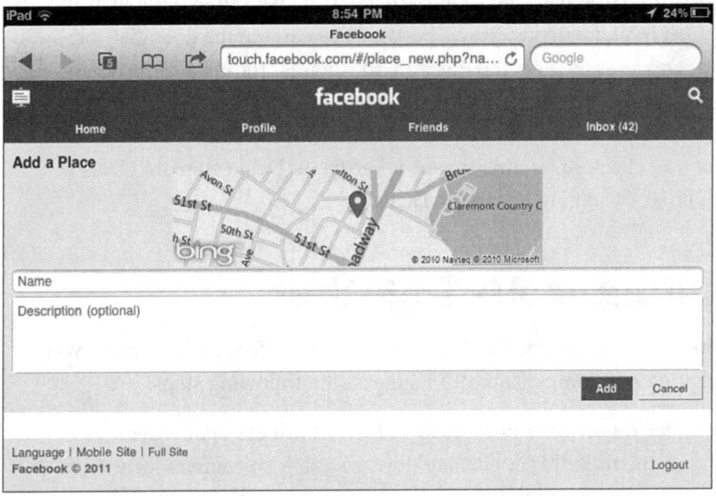

FIGURE 4.7   Add a name and description to go with the map location shown on Facebook.

TIP: **Don't "Out" Private Addresses**

You shouldn't Add a Place that's a private residence unless it's your own. Leave it up to the actual residents to decide whether they want their home address on Facebook Places and, if so, how much biographical information to include. For businesses, though, it's okay to add them—businesses are usually trying to be found.

---

5. For a new place, enter the name and, if you wish, the description.

6. Answer the question, "What are you doing?" with a brief statement. If you want to, also press the **Add Friends Who Are With You** button. A list of your Facebook friends appears; enter part of their name(s) to narrow the list, and then pick the relevant friend(s).

7. Press the **Check in** button.

   Your update appears on the Places check-in page, on your Wall, and in the News Feed of your Facebook friends. The update also appears on the Wall of any friends you checked in with, as well as in their friends' News Feeds. (You can see the potential for embarrassment if the Place in question is, for instance, a neighborhood bar, and your friend called in sick from school or work.)

After you check in, you might see a Facebook Deal (more on Deals in Lesson 10, "Creating Facebook Deals").

Pulling It All Together

So how do you use Facebook's tools with the different elements of your marketing mix, online and off? I suggest the following steps:

▶ **Decide on your best feature.** Every business claims great products, friendly service, and low prices. A convenient location is also prominent in the mix for "brick and mortar" stores and professional offices. However, you should choose the element that you're going to prioritize—literally, put first and mention the most. In the online environment, low prices grab attention, but it can be hard to undercut online retailers. So consider leading with prices and deals, but push quality, service, or your location to help get people in the door.

▶ **Decide on your location strategy.** How far are you trying to reach with your advertising and promotion? Do most of your customers come to you because you're near their homes or offices, or do you have a specialized offering that attracts people from far and wide? You can seek "Likes," and pay for ads, targeted to your local area, or try to reach out more broadly.

▶ **Decide what your key visual is.** You can have a designed logo, like the famous McDonald's "golden arches," a stylized letter M, or an image of the founder or owner, as with Kentucky Fried Chicken's image of the Colonel. Figure 4.8 shows some brand

logos from a "brand of the year" contest. Your key visual is the
core of your brand; the original "branding" was simply burning
an image into a cow's hide, after all. Whichever image you
choose, that's what you'll use on your Facebook Page and in
other advertising.

FIGURE 4.8 Top brands tend to use names, but faces can be good for local
businesses.

- ▶ **Create a website (optional).** Most businesses use their websites
  to carry the main weight of their marketing. The idea is to create
  an attractive, easy to use, easy to search resource that has all your
  key information and promotional material in one place. If you
  don't have a website, though, you can start by creating your fan
  page, and then use it as the basis for a website.

- ▶ **Create your fan page.** The next step is to create your business
  fan page, as described in the next lesson. It's basically a simpli-
  fied version of a typical business website. If you have a website,

your fan page can link to the site to provide more detailed information; if you don't have a website, you can use the fan page as the basis to create one.

- ▶ **Create your Places page.** Create or claim your Places page and make sure the information is accurate. Check in to your own Places page to make sure it works properly. Link to your fan page and your website, if you have one, from your Places page. This is covered in Lessons 5, "Planning Your Fan Page," and 6, "Creating Your Fan Page."

- ▶ **Promote your fan page and Places page.** Encourage people to visit your business fan page and your Places page and to Like them. How to do this for your Places page is covered in Lesson 8, "Expanding and Promoting Your Facebook Page."

- ▶ **Consider Twitter.** At this point, if not before, you might want to consider creating a Twitter account. You can use Twitter to update your fan page for your business, using options that you'll find on the Twitter site. You can use Twitter to promote your Facebook presence as well.

- ▶ **Create Facebook Deals.** Here's where it starts to get interesting. Create Facebook Deals for your business and promote them. Your Deals rely on everything you've done so far—creating and promoting your website (optional), fan page, and Places page. See Lesson 11, "Planning and Targeting Facebook Ads," for more.

- ▶ **Create Facebook Ads.** Advertising on Facebook is fun but potentially expensive. So you want to use the existing free and inexpensive tools—your website, Facebook Page, Places page, and Deals—to learn from and to support your ad when you do run it.

- ▶ **Do it all again.** Building up an online presence as described here is a tremendous learning experience. Having gone through it once, you'll be ready to go through and improve everything— your website, your fan page, your Places page, Facebook Deals, and Facebook Ads.

Summary

In this lesson, you learned how to create a Facebook-first online strategy for your business. You learned how Facebook Pages (also known as "fan pages"), Places pages, Facebook Deals, and Facebook Ads work together. You also learned how to "check in" to a Place on Facebook and steps for getting all the pieces in place. In the next lesson, you learn how to plan your fan page for maximum impact.

LESSON 5

Planning Your Fan Page

In this lesson, you learn about the different elements that make up a fan page via a comparison to a typical business website. You learn how to plan your fan page using the different kinds of content that Facebook supports—freeform text and markup, photos, video, events, reviews, and discussion boards.

Anatomy of a Facebook Page

The first step in building your business' Facebook presence is to decide on your strategy for incorporating Facebook into your overall business and marketing plan, as described in the previous lesson. The next is to fully understand what you're working with, so let's take a look at the basic framework of a Facebook Page and start drafting what you want to see on yours.

Remember that a fan page for a business, organization, or cause is very much like an individual's Profile page, with just a few differences. It's meant to showcase your Wall, which displays the stream of postings that people who have Liked your Facebook Page see in their News Feeds.

NOTE: **A Fan Page as a Work in Progress**
Fan Pages, like full websites, are always works in progress (even more so with a fan page, because your Wall is always getting updated with new posts). However, when you first create your fan page, it should feel fairly complete and coherent. That means, optimally, having three or four tabs, not just one or two, and having good-looking content with everything spelled correctly and working

---

as it should. (No links that don't go anywhere, for instance.) If you're feeling like just doing something quick and dirty, remember the old saying: You only get one chance to make a first impression. Make the first impression for visitors to your Facebook Page a positive one.

Your fan page automatically has Facebook's "look and feel," as shown in Figure 5.1. The major elements of a fan page for business are

FIGURE 5.1   Taking the Sams Publishing Facebook Page apart.

- ▶ **Your logo.** You get a large area in the upper-left area for your logo. Many fan pages use a modified logo that urges the visitor to click the Like button for the page.

- ▶ **Left-hand rail.** Except for your logo, the left side of the page, called the "left-hand rail" by Web designers, is Facebook content. It shows typical fan page links, a few of your followers (the people who have Liked the page), and related photos.

▶ **Title.** The title of your page is the name of your business.

▶ **Like button.** In a way, this is the central focus of the page because getting people to Like your page helps you interact with them regularly on Facebook.

▶ **Tabs.** You specify the tabs shown. The first tab is your Wall, made up simply of postings that you've put up using the business's account. Other tabs can be named whatever you'd like and hold various content, as described in this lesson.

▶ **Page content.** The content underneath each tab is different, which you specify. Your Wall content is built one posting at a time and also includes Likes and comments from people. These bring your Wall to life, so try to get comments. Other pages can be standard Facebook content or can be semi-customized.

▶ **Right-hand rail.** The right-hand rail is made up of Facebook Ads, often targeted to people who advertisers assume are likely to visit a fan page of this type.

You can also add extra tabs to your Wall that hold various kinds of content. With the additional tabs, a Facebook Page is like a fairly simple website within Facebook. The Facebook Page has several links down the left-hand side, and each link contains a single page of content.

> **NOTE: Consider Creating a Storyboard**
>
> Consider creating a pencil sketch, or "storyboard," for the Wall of your Facebook Page and the sections in it. Then create a separate storyboard for each section. List the modules you want to put in each section, as described in this lesson, and briefly describe the purpose of each. Discuss the results with anyone who's interested. You'll get a much better fan page this way, and you'll be done much faster than if you just dive in and start entering stuff.

Planning Your Fan Page

If you're a solo act, you can plan your fan page all by yourself. If you're part of a larger business, you should get input from others. In either case, you can also reach outside of your business, to customers, other business owners, and knowledgeable friends and family for ideas and feedback.

Your Wall will evolve by itself, as described in the next section. As you plan your fan page, though, you'll want to launch the page with a few other sections, each having suitable content. The sections can be the same as or different from those on your website.

TIP: **Don't Copy Your Website onto Facebook**

People don't like to leave Facebook once they're in it, so it can be tempting to more or less copy your website onto Facebook. That way, people will get the content without having to leave. This approach, though, doesn't take full advantage of what Facebook does well. Emphasize social, highly visual, interactive content in Facebook. Then add in the top couple most-used elements from your website, which might include contact information and key technical support information. For other elements, link people to your website.

Facebook allows you to create the content for your fan page using a kind of drag-and-drop interface that I cover in some detail in the next lesson. You put boxes onscreen and then specify what kind of content goes into them. The kinds of content are described in general in this lesson—to help you with planning—and in more detail in the next lesson.

Following are some ideas for choosing and filling in tabs for your Facebook Page—intended only as a starting point for a brainstorming session. After you decide what you want to do, the information in the next lesson will help you do it.

Typical Website Tabs

A typical website includes tabs that you can adapt for your fan page:

▶ **Home tab.** For your fan page, your Home tab is your Wall. You can choose a different default tab if you like, though. The Amazon.com fan page (shown in Lesson 1, "Introducing Facebook for Business") has an entire tab just to encourage people to click the Like button for the page and made that page the default page for visitors. The page had about 500,000 Likes last I checked.

- **Contact information.** Difficult-to-find contact information is the number one complaint of visitors to traditional websites. Make complete contact information—including the URL of your website; your phone number; a map; and anything else that helps people reach you—super easy to find on your Facebook Page.

- **About the company.** This is information about who you are, where you're based, and so on. You can jazz this up for Facebook; include something interesting about your philosophy, feature a quote from a younger employee, and so on.

- **Press releases and announcements.** Have a dedicated place for news such as new hires, promotions, events, and so on. You can tie this into the Facebook Profile for the business—an alert goes out as a status update and links back to your fan page for more information.

- **Products and/or services.** You want to sell, of course, but you should use a lighter touch on Facebook. So consider including simple highlights of what you sell, perhaps in the form of fun facts. Choose an approach that's likely to promote engagement in the form of feedback and comments, not just sales. (You're likely to end up with more sales that way.)

The Canadian arm of the Technology Group for Pearson, the publishers of this book, has brought all these elements together in a successful example of this kind of site, as shown in Figure 5.2.

If you do include some of these basic sections from your website in your Facebook Page, consider livening them up a bit. For instance, you could put your contact information in a section called Get in Touch. Products, if they have an element of fun to them, could be called Stuff. The presentation might also be different—heavy on the photos, light on the technical specifications.

FIGURE 5.2   Pearson Technology Group Canada has the Web formula right.

Freeform Pages Using FBML

When you create a typical web page, you use HTML—HyperText Markup Language. This is a kind of code embedded in the text on your Web page that controls how the page is structured.

You might not see the actual HTML, though. Many web design tools hide HTML from you and allow you to use word-processing type controls to bold words, create bulleted or numbered lists, and so on. The design tool actually creates the HTML code to make it all happen for you.

Facebook also allows you to create freeform content within your tabs, using a version of HTML called Facebook Markup Language, or FBML. An FBML page can be up to 760 pixels wide—more than half the width of a typical widescreen laptop (which is typically 1280 pixels)—and can even have Flash animations embedded in it.

You can use FBML for simple stuff too, however. The Pep Boys fan page has a Careers tab that's just one big graphic, as shown in Figure 5.3. You

FIGURE 5.3   The Careers tab on Pep Boys' Facebook Page...

click a button on the graphic to go to the Careers section on the Pep Boys home page, shown in Figure 5.4.

Photos and Video

Photos and video are a huge source of content on Facebook, even more than on the Web as a whole. Photos give you a chance to show yourself and your business in a more relaxed, casual light. A steady stream of new photos makes your site much more lively. You can post photos one at a time, as status updates, which keeps your Wall up to date as well.

Web-quality photos aren't as "fancy" as printed photos; a pretty poor-quality photo can look fine online, even if it looks terrible as a color print. And Facebook inherently promotes a culture of experimentation and fun with photographs. So I'm not going to spend much time here on the proper use of Facebook photos in your online presence. I do encourage

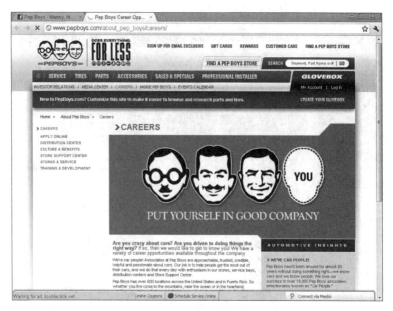

FIGURE 5.4   ...takes you to the Careers area on the Pep Boys website.

you, though, to upload photos on an ongoing basis and to experiment with how you use them.

Pep Boys has a photos page, shown in Figure 5.5, that's very much in the Facebook spirit—not overproduced, a lot of fun, local, and even silly in spots. You can see past Pep Boys logos used on their fan page in the Profile Pictures section.

It's not always easy for a business to cut loose like Pep Boys has done, but if you can manage it, your customers are likely to feel more connected to the people behind your business image.

Videos are a whole other ball of wax. You can use them for casual updates, just as you might with photos, or create expensive-looking, carefully lit, professionally scripted presentations or content. People are using video in every way imaginable these days, from the talking cats of I Can Has Cheezburger? to professionally staged seminars. (To see the lolcats of I Can Has Cheezburger?, visit http://icanhascheezburger.com.) You can, too.

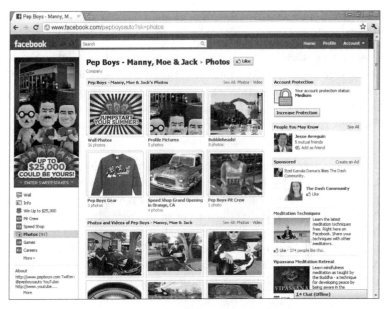

FIGURE 5.5   Pep Boys has fun with photos, and so can you.

There are two main things to be aware of when using video in your fan page. The first is that in their online behavior, people are sorting themselves along a continuum from video fans to videophobes. I, personally, don't like video clips or podcasts much; I can't go through them quickly in the way that I can scan a page of text and then read it again more slowly only if it's worthwhile. However, I have friends who love video online; people often send me links to 60- or 90-minute online lectures and shows.

The upshot is that you almost have to put some video on your Facebook Page if you want to engage your whole potential audience, because that's the main thing some people are looking for. However, you also have to provide the same content that's in the video in other ways as well, because some people won't watch a video clip no matter how great or important you say it is.

In addition to video reaching some audiences very well and others poorly or not at all, you need to be aware that video is potentially expensive to make. Some people can pick up their mobile phones or use a webcam to shoot short, interesting clips that look "good enough" for web use. Others, though, go the full professional production route for their online videos.

Your own approach to video depends on the talent you have (or that the people around you have), your business, and your goals. I can only suggest that you find ways to use video regularly in your Facebook presence, including in your fan page. Creating a section called Videos on your Facebook Page and seeding it with an early entry or two is one way to pressure yourself to create and post videos.

The Videos page of the Pep Boys site is shown in Figure 5.6. At this writing, this page is not quite as strong as the rest of Pep Boys' Facebook presence. There aren't that many videos, but you can imagine that the demand for videos from the customers of an auto parts chain might not be immense. The Videos by Others section only has one video, and this looks like a big opportunity for a marketing push on Facebook and YouTube. Nothing wrong here—just somewhat of a missed opportunity. You may be able to do better in a Videos tab for your own site.

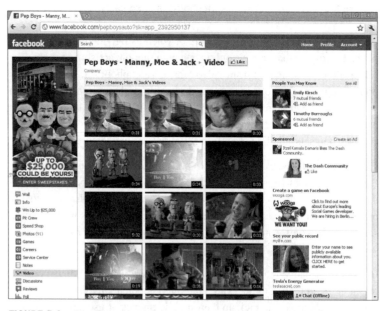

FIGURE 5.6   Pep Boys has several commercials in its Videos tab.

Events, Reviews, and Discussion Boards

Fan pages offers three special types of functionality that you can use in your fan page tabs: Events; Reviews; and Discussion Boards.

Each of these is valuable in its own right, but only in certain cases. To have an Events area to work, you actually have to have events. You can call having a sale an event, but most people will expect something a bit less commercial and more educational or fun. So if you do have events, by all means, use the Facebook Events module to present them on Facebook.

You might also want to use a site like Meetup.com or a service like Evite.com to manage events, instead of or alongside the Facebook event. This makes the event accessible to people who aren't on Facebook, or don't use it much. The Facebook version can be good for helping inspire people to bring along their friends who are also frequent users of Facebook.

Putting discussion boards up on your Facebook Page for your business is a bit risky because an area like this is likely to attract three kinds of input: praise; criticism; and spam, such as ads for other people's business and even obscenities. So if you do put up such a board, you have to be ready to get rid of the real junk and respond to the criticism quickly and forthrightly. Doing all this is very good business practice, but it takes work and courage.

Pep Boys has a discussion board on their Facebook Page, as shown in Figure 5.7. Pep Boys is very responsive to comments.

Allowing people to post reviews of your products and services is tricky as well. Amazon.com is the world's expert in managing online reviews, and they get a lot of value out of them. But, for your own business, do you really want that kind of freely voiced opinion taking place about the products you sell? Books, which is where Amazon started, are famous as objects of discussion and debate—even of book burnings. The items you sell might not be as review-friendly as books.

Reviews are similar to discussion boards. They can be good for having your fan page visitors form a community of sorts, helping each other with technical support, recipes, or whatever's appropriate to your business. Managing either discussion boards or reviews, though, can be a hassle.

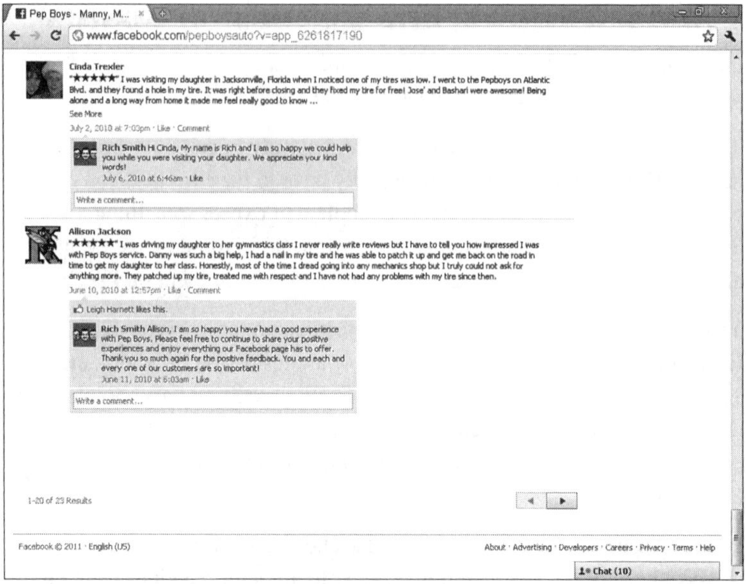

FIGURE 5.7   Pep Boys gives its customers a chance to sound off.

CAUTION: **Scrubbing Your Facebook Page**

One of the great things about Facebook is that you can easily remove people's comments from your Facebook Page. This is pretty much necessary for getting rid of obscenities, hate speech, and other stuff that's just off the wall (pun intended). Problematic comments can appear as comments on your status updates as well as in areas such as discussion boards.

Do remove comments that are clearly over the line. Be cautious, however, about removing content that you simply dislike or that's in marginally poor taste. A bit of debate and disagreement on your Facebook Page can help make it lively and interesting. Exactly where to draw the line, though, is up to you.

Events, reviews, and discussion boards all imply a lot of work after the initial Facebook setup to make them a success. You have to hope that people participate, monitor the way they participate, and so on. Do use one or more of these modules if they make sense for the way you run your business; don't add them just for fun. Whatever you do, be ready to do the work to back it up.

Summary

In this lesson, you learned about the different elements that make up a Facebook Page in comparison to a typical business website. You learned how to plan your fan page using the different kinds of content that Facebook supports—freeform text and markup, photos, video, events, reviews, and discussion boards. In the next lesson, you'll learn how to create your fan page.

LESSON 6

Creating Your Fan Page

In this lesson, you create your business fan page. You start by choosing the name for your page, which is reflected in its URL. You then learn how to sign up for your page.

Checking if Your Business Name Is in Use

Your Facebook Page is an important part of your business's marketing strategy, and nothing's more important than the name.

I start this lesson by helping you get your business name into your Facebook URL. So if your business name is Floyd's Friendly Fones, you may well be able to have the most sensible URL for your Facebook Page: www.facebook.com/Floyds-Friendly-Fones. That would look great on a business card, wouldn't it? And a lot better than a computer-generated URL, something like www.facebook.com/pages/as12d9gsa0k.

> NOTE: **Take Your Time with Naming**
> Some of the biggest regrets I hear from businesspeople have to do with their business names and their Web addresses. It can be the business name itself; the URL they've chosen, which may or may not reflect the business name; or a blog name or Twitter handle. In addition to regrets, people also get themselves into real problems trying to rename the business itself, the website, and so on. Now Facebook Pages comes along to give you yet another chance to get your business name right—or frustratingly wrong.

The friendly kind of URL is called a vanity URL. It's like a vanity license plate—HOT STUF, say, instead of 2 BJZ 157 (using the format for license plates here in California).

There are two small flies in the otherwise useful ointment:

▶ It takes a bit of thought to come up with exactly the name you want Facebook to use, but Facebook asks you for the name within a short series of otherwise trivial steps. So it's easy to enter a name you'll regret later.

▶ Many good names are already taken (though not Floyd's Friendly Fones—I checked).

In this section I also take you through the reasons for using a vanity URL, tell you how to find the right name to use, and give you some tips in case your first choice of a name is already taken.

Why Use a Vanity URL?

Vanity URLs are extremely popular. A nonvanity URL just confuses people and makes their lives difficult. A vanity URL is easy for people to remember, reinforces the name of your business with your users, and is easy for search engines to find.

Facebook takes the name you enter and adds dashes between the words to make the last part of your URL. Putting dashes into your business's name when creating the URL might not be everyone's first choice. However, it makes the URL very search engine-friendly.

Interestingly, Facebook used to limit vanity URLs to Facebook Pages that had at least 100 followers. However, this caused businesses a problem. A business would launch a Facebook Page with an obscure URL; put that on stationery, promotions, and so on at launch; and had to work hard to get people to come to their page, given the URL was so obscure.

So then after a Facebook Page with an obscure URL did, with effort, reach 100 fans, the business would then get the treasured vanity URL—and have to redo all their marketing materials and re-educate the public to use the new URL.

So Facebook now gives you the vanity URL right up front. This is great and as it should be, but it means that you need to understand what's going on with the URL before you create your Facebook Page.

Just What Name Should You Use?

Figuring out just what name to use can be complicated for some business owners or managers. You might have a long business name that won't fit conveniently at the top of your fan page, nor in a URL. Names that look cute on a sign might not translate so well to the world of the Web.

When you set up your fan page, you enter a name for it. Facebook takes the name, replaces spaces between words with dashes, and uses that as the last part of your page's URL.

One big concern that relates to both web search and URLs is what you might call "spellability." That is, if you say the name out loud, can people then spell it correctly when typing it into a search engine? My full name, Floyd Earl Smith, is fine, if a bit odd; but a name like my father's old restaurant—Eric Stromfield, Phurrier—is going to cause confusion and mistakes. (My dad renamed the restaurant soon after taking ownership.)

In addition to a spellable name, you want a reasonably short name. This is good for memorability, searchability, and creating a reasonable URL for Facebook. (The URL is always going to start with 17 characters, www. facebook.com/, so you want as few additional characters as reasonably possible.)

You also want a business name, and therefore a Facebook vanity URL, that exactly matches any web URL you have, if at all possible. (However, it probably won't be an exact match, at any rate, because Facebook puts dashes in the name.) This makes it easy for users; they go to www. floydsfriendlyfones.com for the website and www.facebook.com/ Floyds-Friendly-Fones.com for the Facebook Page. This can be clumsy, though, if you've chosen a website URL that doesn't exactly match your business name.

Here's a brief checklist of what to look out for in choosing the business name to use for your Facebook Page, which will be transformed by Facebook into your vanity URL:

- ▶ **Make it accurate.** Use your exact business name if at all possible.

- ▶ **Make it short.** Consider shortening a long business name if needed to fit on the page and to create a memorable URL.

▶ **Make it guessable.** Anyone who knows the name of your business (and knows to put dashes between the words) should be able
to guess your Facebook URL.

▶ **Make it consistent.** The business name on your Facebook Page
and in the URL for that page should be consistent with the URL
for your business website.

Note that not all of these "musts" necessarily point to the same answer. If
there are several possibilities, list them all, along with their plusses and
minuses. Discuss it with people who know you and your business. Ask
them what they think your Facebook URL should be. Use the information
you gather to help you decide your next step.

If the "perfect" name for your business is already in use, there are ways to
get to a really good name without breaking too many rules. If you have a
local business, consider adding the town or area name to your domain name.

Try not to make the name too long, though. This is easy in San Francisco
or San Diego, for instance, because you can use the initials SF or SD—not
so easy in Milwaukee or Philadelphia.

You can also add a street name, part or all of your personal name, or some
other piece of relevant information. Don't just add digits or random characters; people won't be able to remember them, and it won't make sense.

There's a lot of information on the Web about choosing a good domain
name. One of the more helpful articles I found is on the site Domain
Superstar at www.domainsuperstar.com. The site has tools to help you get
a great domain name.

The article, "25 Rules for Choosing a Domain Name," is quite extensive
and helpful. Check it out at: www.domainsuperstar.com/how-to-choose-a-
domain-name.

Checking Out Your Candidates

All of this work and thought should conclude with one business name that
you really want to use for your Facebook Page or a few candidates. Now,

for each name you have to see if it's already in use. You want to check if it's in use on Facebook and if it's in use on the Web.

> NOTE: **Using Multiple URLs**
>
> Let's say that the name of your business is Floyd's Friendly Fones and that you can use the URL www.facebook.com/Floyds-Friendly-Fones for Facebook. However, you may have your web page at a different kind of URL, such as www.foneworld.com. If so, there's no need to change your Web URL, which is hard or even impossible to do; too many people know the old version. The answer is simple: buy several URLs, such as www.floydsfriendlyfones.com and www.floyds-friendly-fones.com and point them to your main website. That way, people who guess your website URL based on your Facebook Page URL or your business name will get where they want to go (which is also where you want them to go!).

So to get cracking on setting up your name, follow these steps:

1. First, check the Web (unless you're already using the business name as your website URL). Open a Web browser and go to a domain name checking service. The most popular registrar is GoDaddy, at www.godaddy.com.

2. Type in the business name as a URL, with www. at the beginning and .com at the end. So for Floyd's Friendly Fones, type in **www.floydsfriendlyfones.com**. Also try the name with dashes, as in **www.floyds-friendly-fones.com**.

   Results will appear. You want both versions, with dashes and without, to be available. An example from GoDaddy is shown in Figure 6.1.

3. Now try the name that you want to use for Facebook. Simply try the business name you want as part of a Facebook URL, like so: **www.facebook.com/floyds-friendly-fones**.

   If a page shows up, the business name is already in use as a Facebook Page. If no page shows up, the business name, and related domain name within Facebook is available.

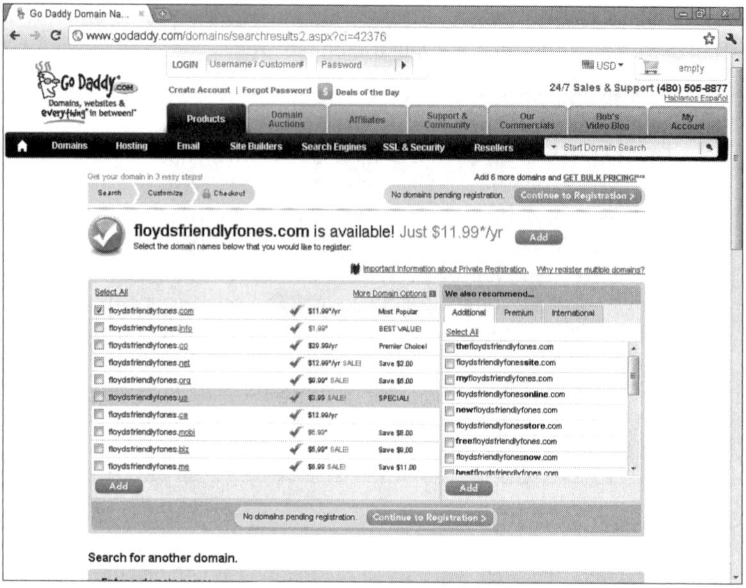

FIGURE 6.1   Searching for a domain name can be both fun and frustrating.

4. This process will probably give you ideas; write down any new ideas you have as you go along.

5. Write down the results for each name. (It can be very frustrating to forget which names you've tried and which names you haven't.) Repeat steps 1 through 3 until you've tried all the names you started with, as well as any new ideas that come up.

When you're done, you'll have one or more candidates for a name.

Making Your Choice

If you have a clear name for your business, and it's available as both a Facebook Page name and a Web URL—or if you already have the Web URL—then you're done. It's obvious which name to use for your Facebook Page.

If not, take a bit more time with naming. Run your suggested names by several people. Remember that the name you choose will appear as both your business name at the top of your Facebook Page, with spaces instead of dashes and as part of the URL for your Facebook Page, with dashes instead of spaces. Also you may use the same name as part of a Web URL, with neither dashes nor spaces.

Take all three forms of the name—plain English, as part of a Facebook Page URL, and as part of a Web URL—and write them down. Here's an example:

Plain English: Floyd's Friendly Fones

Facebook Page URL: www.facebook.com/Floyds-Friendly-Fones

Web URL: www.floydsfriendlyfones.com

CAUTION: **Domain Name Fever**

It's very easy to get caught up in buying domain names to protect business ideas that you have, but it might never amount to anything. It's a very good idea to buy one or a few domain names to protect a real, existing, money-making business. But it's not so good an idea to tie up domain names just because you might want to start, say, a friendly phone company one day.

Write out each version of the name in this three-part format and run them by some people. Get them talking about what they do and don't like. If you get new ideas from this process, repeat the steps in the previous section to check the new names out and see if they're available.

When you're done, you'll—finally!—have a name ready and waiting to use when you create your Facebook Page.

Signing Up for Your Page

Now it's time to actually create the Facebook Page for your business. Don't worry; it's a fun, flexible process, and you can always change or improve your Facebook Page. (The flexibility only goes so far—you have to fill in all the fields, for instance.) At the end, you're likely to be quite proud to have a business presence on Facebook.

Follow these steps to sign up:

1. Sign into Facebook.

Your News Feed appears.

2. Scroll down to the bottom of the page and find the links in the lower-right corner. Click the **Advertising** link.

The Facebook Ads page, shown in Figure 6.2, appears.

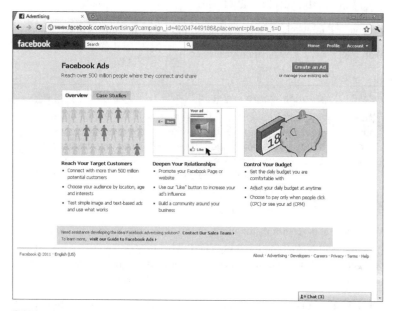

FIGURE 6.2 The Facebook Ads page starts the advertising process.

3. If you want to learn more about Facebook Ads right now, click the **Case Studies** tab.

4. On the original Overview tab in the middle of the page under Deepen Your Relationships, click the **Facebook Page** link.

You'll see a mini-site for creating your Facebook Page, as shown in Figure 6.3. Consider reviewing the other tabs before proceeding.

FIGURE 6.3 Facebook offers you a mini-site for creating your Facebook Page.

5. Click the **Create a Page** button.

   The Create a Page page, shown in Figure 6.4, appears.

6. Click the button for **Local Business or Place of Interest**.

   The button rather cleverly changes to a request for basic information: category, name, address, and phone number, as shown in Figure 6.5.

7. Choose the category from the pull-down list.

   You might want to discuss your choices for the category with others to make sure you select the best option. (Try to avoid choosing "Local Business" because it's too broad.)

   The choices are: Airport; Arts/Entertainment/Nightlife; Attractions/Things to Do; Automotive; Bank/Financial Services;

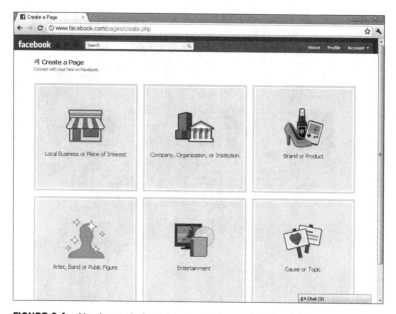

FIGURE 6.4   You have choices as you start your Facebook Page.

Bar; Business Services; Church/Religious Organization; Club; Community/Government; Concert Venue; Education; Event Planning/Event Services; Food/Grocery; Health/Medical/ Pharmacy; Home Improvement; Hospital/Clinic; Hotel; Landmark; Library; Local Business; Movie Theater; Museum/Art Gallery; Pet Services; Professional Services; Public Places; Real Estate; Restaurant/Café; School; Shopping/Retail; Spas/Beauty/ Personal Care; Sports Venue; Sports/Recreation/Activities; Tours/Sightseeing; Transit Stop; Transportation; University.

8. Enter the name for the business or place of interest.

The name you enter will be used to create a "vanity URL" for your Facebook Page. For instance, if you enter "The Olde Rubber Ducky Shoppe" as the page name, your URL will be www.facebook.com/The-Olde-Rubber-Ducky-Shoppe. (The dashes are annoying, but they help make the URL easy to find using search engines.) You might wish to use a shorter name that

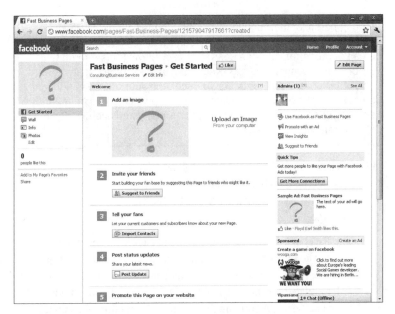

FIGURE 6.5   Your new page appears—empty at first.

still gets the point across, such as "Rubber Ducky." See the discussion at the beginning of this lesson for details.

9. Enter the business address: street address, city, state, and ZIP code.

If you run your business out of your home, you might not want to publicize the address on Facebook in order to reduce the potential for identity theft.

10. Enter the phone number.

As with the risk of listing a personal address, if you're using your personal phone number for your business, you might not want to enter it on Facebook.

CAUTION: **Avoid Over-Sharing**

One of the great things about new technology such as Facebook is that it makes it very easy to start up a business with very little capital outlay, such as using your home as your office. However, avoid putting personal information of this type on Facebook. So if you're using your personal phone, home address, and/or your personal email address for your business, consider leaving this information off of your Facebook Page to avoid identity theft, email spammers, and other privacy problems. As you scale up your business and get a separate phone number, address or P.O. box, email address, and so on, you can add that new information into your Facebook Pages at any time with no problem.

11. If you wish, review the Facebook Pages Terms by clicking the **Review the Facebook Terms** link. Also, if you wish to review the overall Facebook terms, click the Terms link at the bottom of the page.

The Facebook Pages Terms are a single page with about a dozen terms. The overall Facebook Terms are about three pages of quite readable text and well worth your time to review. The Terms also link to related documents, including Facebook's Privacy Policy, Payment Terms, Advertising Guidelines, Promotions Guidelines, and others. Several of these may also be of interest to you now or in the future.

12. Click the checkbox next to the words, **I agree to the Facebook Pages Terms**.

13. Click the **Get Started** button.

Your page appears, similar to that shown in Figure 6.5. Note that it includes tabs—Get Started, to start filling in your Page; Wall, for your status updates; Info, with information you'll add in the next lesson; and +, for additional tabs.

Instructions for filling in the information on your new Facebook fan page are found in the following two lessons.

CAUTION: **Be Sure You Are the Legitimate Owner**

Before creating a page for a business, be sure that you're the legitimate owner or acting with that person's permission. Take the warnings that Facebook gives about this seriously; Facebook frequently removes content that violates its policies and bans users who have, in its view, committed violations. Trying to get such a decision reversed is difficult.

NOTE: **A Facebook Page as a Work in Progress**

Facebook Pages, like full websites, are always works in progress (even more so with a Facebook Page because your Wall is always getting updated with new posts). However, before you tell people about your new Facebook page, it should be fairly complete and coherent. That means, optimally, having four or five tabs, not just the default tabs, and having good-looking content with everything spelled correctly and working as it should—no links that don't go anywhere, for instance. You should even have some status updates on your Wall before you announce the page widely. If you're feeling like just doing something quick and dirty, think twice and commit to making sure your visitors' initial impressions are as positive and informative as they can be.

Summary

In this lesson, you created your business Facebook Page. You started by choosing the name to use for your page, which is reflected in the URL for the page. You then learned how to sign up for your page. In the next lesson, you learn how to continue setting up your fan page.

LESSON 7

Setting Up Your Business Fan Page

In this lesson, you learn how to manage core settings for your Facebook fan page. This includes basic information about your business, adding a profile photo or logo, adding and managing apps for your business fan page (as opposed to your personal page), and changing mobile settings.

Creating Core Settings for Your Business Fan Page

Just like your personal Facebook page, the fan page for your business has permissions and settings that control how it works. They're fairly simple but important.

This lesson takes you through the core settings and their implications. By getting these settings right the first time and knowing where to go to change something when you need to, you'll be way ahead in managing your Facebook presence.

Entering Basic Information

Start by editing basic information about your page.

Follow these steps:

1. Sign in to Facebook.

2. In the left-hand rail, under Apps and Marketplace, click the **More** link.

    Links for Games, Photos, Notes, Ads and Pages, and Links appear.

3. Click Ads and Pages.

    A list of pages that you can administer appears.

4. Under your page's name, click the **Edit Page** link.

    The Basic Information area appears, as shown in Figure 7.1.

5. Check the Name for your page.

    This is the name that will display across the top of your Facebook Page; you won't want to change it unless you change your business name—to keep it consistent with your URL.

6. Enter the business's address and, if asked, the hours of operation, street address, city or town, and ZIP code.

    As mentioned in the previous lesson, if you run your business out of your home, you might not want to publicize the address on Facebook to reduce the potential for identity theft.

7. Enter information about the company by filling in a sentence in the About field. And in the Description field you can write some text, perhaps one paragraph, which summarizes your company, a basic overview of its products or services or maybe your mission statement. General Information (which should be brief and to the

point), Price Range, Parking, and Public Transit information are also fields that you can fill in to give people a better understanding of your business.

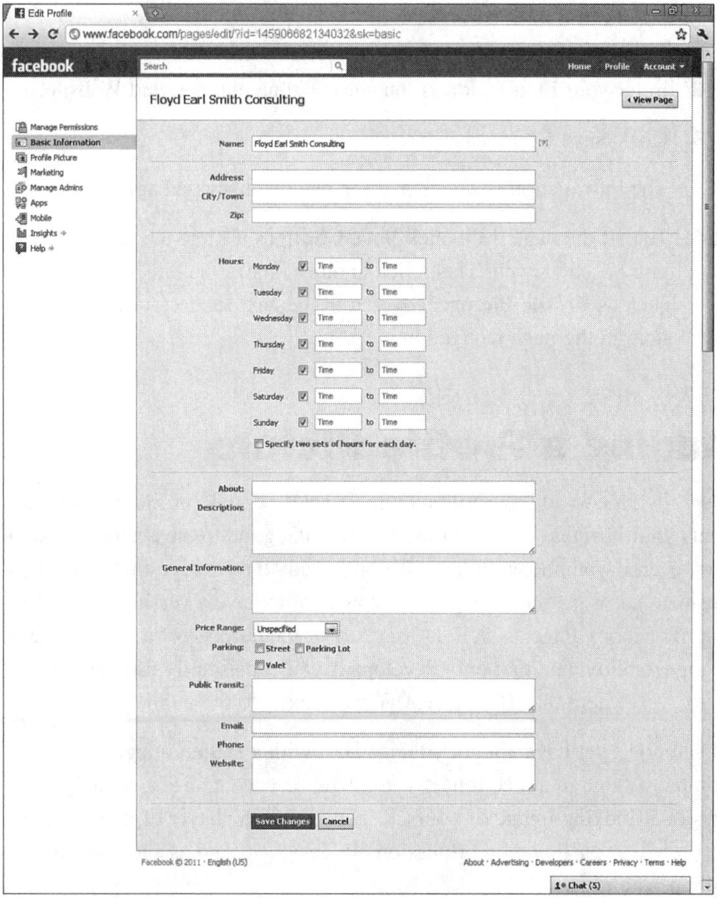

FIGURE 7.1 The Basic Information area for your Page is important.

TIP: **Print It to Edit It**

Any time text needs to be carefully written and/or edited, you should print it out and review the printed version. Printed text is easier to read, so people write and edit better from a printed original than from an onscreen version.

---

8. Enter your Email address, business Phone number, and Website.

9. Click **Save Changes**.

   The information is saved, and the page is displayed again.

10. To exit the page, first click **Save Changes** if there are changes you haven't saved. Then click another link in the left-hand rail, such as **Profile Picture**, covered in the next section, or another item in the page navigation.

Adding a Profile Picture

Now it's time to add a profile picture. Your Facebook profile picture represents your business to the world. As such, it's good to have a logo of some sort, even if you change it later. If you already have a logo that is used on business cards, signage, and so on, you want to have a version of that for your Facebook Page as well. (A big part of the purpose of a logo is instant recognizability, and that only develops if you consistently use the same logo everywhere that you present your business to the public.)

If you don't yet have a logo, you can start with a simple image of your company name in a nice font if you'd like, or you can use a suitably professional-looking image of yourself. However, whichever of these you begin with, you'll want a professionally designed logo as soon as reasonably possible.

NOTE: **Differentiating Your Page**

Facebook presents your Facebook Page using the Facebook look and feel. This promotes a high comfort level for users, and saves you a lot of trouble and potential expense, since you don't have to create your own look and feel. However, it also makes it hard for you to differentiate your page. As a result, your logo or photo, the apps you choose, and your status updates, among other elements, all have to work hard and work together to communicate your business' personality and goals.

Follow these steps to get your image loaded:

1. If you don't already have one, create a file with an image of your logo or a suitable photo. For photos, JPEG format is usually best; for files with text, PNG or GIF are the safest choices.

   Many people use JPEG for images with text, but this usually causes ugly bleeding of the text into the background and can cause color gradations to appear blocky as well.

2. Go to the editing area for your Facebook Page, as described in the previous section, steps 1 through 4.

3. Click the **Profile Picture** link.

   The profile picture area appears.

4. Click the button, **Choose File**. (You can also choose **Take a Picture** to take a picture with a Webcam, but such an image is unlikely to be suitable for business purposes.)

   The Choose File to Open dialog appears.

5. Navigate to the folder that contains your picture file and click the **Open** button as shown in Figure 7.2.

   Your picture appears on the page.

Adding and Managing Apps

You get a chance here to add apps to your fan page. Look for apps that fit your specific business and that would be attractive to your customers. This is an important part of differentiating your Facebook presence within the uniform Facebook look and feel.

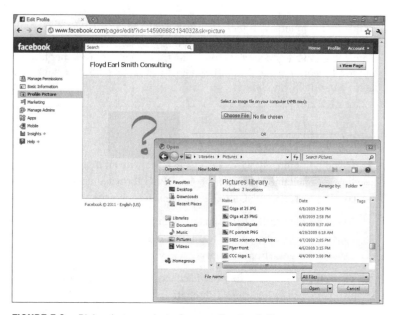

FIGURE 7.2   Pick a logo or photo for your Facebook Page.

Follow these steps for apps:

1. Go to the editing area for your Facebook Page, as described earlier in the section "Entering Basic Information," steps 1 through 4, and click the **Apps** link.

Your list of Added Apps along with an area called Apps You May Like appears, as shown in Figure 7.3.

2. In the Added Apps area, click the **Edit Settings** link. Review the settings and make sure that they're appropriate for the way you want to use the app on the Facebook Page.

3. Click the **Browse more applications** link in the Apps You May Like section.

The All Apps page appears, as shown previously in Figure 3.3. Review Lesson 3, "Finding and Installing Apps," for information about finding and adding apps, including apps specifically relevant to your business.

FIGURE 7.3   Add new apps here.

Changing Mobile Settings and Your URL

Facebook has several mobile settings. Some are informational, and others you can change.

> NOTE: **No Facebook App for the iPad So Far**
>
> Facebook steadfastly refuses to join tens of thousands of other software developers to provide an app for the iPad. This is odd, though, because the iPhone Facebook app is so good. Instead, Mark Zuckerberg has stated that the iPad is "not a mobile platform"—which is news to its users—and can best be accessed via the portable version of Facebook at www.touch.mobile.com.

Pay careful attention to these settings, as they affect how easy it is to keep your Facebook Page updated while you're on the move. Follow these steps to check and use the mobile settings:

1. Go to the editing area for your Facebook Page, as described earlier in the section "Entering Basic Information," steps 1 through 4, and click the **Mobile** link.

    An eclectic list of mobile settings appears, as shown in Figure 7.4.

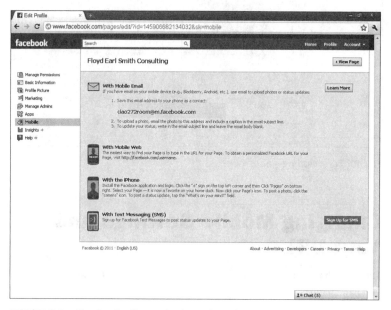

FIGURE 7.4   Facebook offers a hodgepodge of mobile settings for your page.

2. Examine the first setting, With Mobile Email. Save the email address given; use it for updating your fan page with new photos and status updates.

    The email address given will be used to convert email messages from your mobile device into photo or text-only status updates for your Facebook Page.

3. (Recommended.) Try sending status updates to your Facebook
   Page using the email address given. Send a photo via email to the
   address given, with the caption in the subject line. Send an email
   with a text-only status update in the subject line and the body of
   the message blank. Confirm that both techniques work as
   intended.

4. Examine the next setting, With Mobile Web. It may allow you to
   make a one-time-only change to the Facebook URL for your
   Facebook Page, as described in the Note.

NOTE: **Changing Your Fan Page URL**

At this writing, you can only make a change to your Facebook URL if
your Facebook Page has more than 25 fans (people who've
pressed the Like button for it), and any change you make is perma-
nent. See Lesson 6, "Creating Your Fan Page," for information
about how to set up your Page so it has a vanity URL in the first
place, and for information about how to change the URL if you do
have 25 Likes and decide to take advantage of this opportunity.

---

5. Examine the instructions under With the iPhone.

   Follow the instructions given to use the iPhone Facebook App to
   create an icon that makes it easy to update your Facebook Page
   from your iPhone.

TIP: **Use the iPhone App for iPad**

If you wish, you can use the iPhone Facebook app on your iPad. It
looks strange, whether you leave it in small mode (the same size
as on the iPhone) or push the 2x button to enlarge it, which is
called "pixel doubling." However, the easy-to-use functionality for
updating Pages is worth the hassle of using an iPhone app on the
iPad.

---

6. Examine the description under the heading, With Text Messaging (SMS). If you wish to enable text message updates from you to your fan page from one specific phone, click the **Sign Up for SMS** button.

A dialog appears asking you to enter the country and mobile carrier for your phone.

Note that this capability is separate from updating your Facebook Page using email, as described in step 2 or by using the Facebook site on your mobile phone. If more than one person will be updating your Facebook Page, consider reserving the SMS capability for someone who doesn't have a smartphone or who prefers using SMS updating to using email, a mobile web browser, or an app to do it.

7. To continue setting up Facebook Texts, choose your Country and Mobile Carrier from the pull-down lists. Click **Next** when finished.

When you click Next, the dialog shown in Figure 7.5 appears.

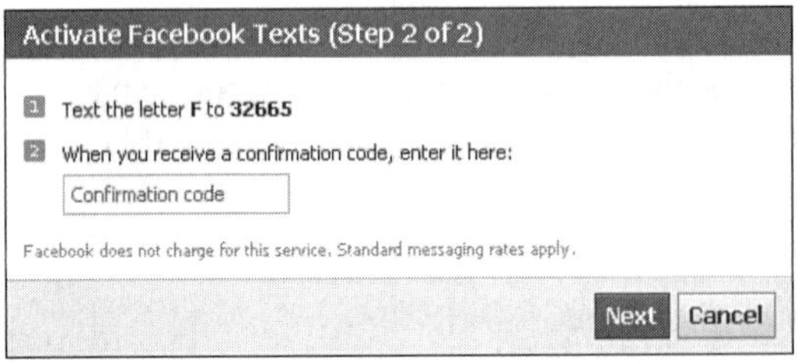

FIGURE 7.5   Facebook asks you to confirm your mobile number for Facebook Texts.

8. To finish setting up Facebook Texts, text the letter shown to the number shown. When you receive a confirmation code, enter it in the field indicated. Click **Next** when done.

The specific mobile phone you used is now activated for sending text messages as text-only status updates to your Facebook Page.

Summary

In this lesson you learned how to manage core settings for your Facebook fan page. This includes basic information about your business, adding a profile photo or logo, adding and managing apps for your business Facebook fan page (as opposed to your personal page), and managing mobile settings. In the next lesson, you learn how to expand your fan page further and how to promote it.

LESSON 8

Expanding and Promoting Your Fan Page

In this lesson, you learn when and how to invite people to your Facebook Page, how to build the Wall of your page through status updates—text, photos, links, and video—and how to manage the Info, Photos, Discussions, and other tabs.

Waiting to Send Out Invitations

When you kick off your Facebook fan page for your business, Facebook first displays a page called "Get Started," which makes it easy for you to invite people to come to your fan page right at the beginning when there's nothing on it.

This makes a lot of sense—for Facebook. All the people you invite who aren't yet using Facebook, or who are users but aren't very active, might just join or get more active because of your invitation. So Facebook wants you to reach out to as many people as possible as quickly as possible.

The trouble with this approach is that it's not very good for you from a business perspective. Inviting a lot of people to come to your fan page when it's not set up, or doesn't have any content, is like inviting people to come visit your new restaurant when it's still under construction and the chef hasn't worked his first day yet. Not very many people are likely to come back.

So I recommend, instead, that you do the same thing with your Facebook Page that you'd do with opening a restaurant:

- ▶ **Get it set up nicely and make it pop.** Remember that your goal is to make a great first impression.

▶ **Invite a few close friends in.** Invite them to try it. Make sure they Like the page so they get status updates, then ask them to comment on a status update or two. Find out from them what they like and don't like.

▶ **Make a few improvements.** Use the feedback you get to improve your fan page. Focus on improvements that encourage people to Like the page when they visit.

▶ **Then—and only then—invite everyone else.** They'll get a great first impression, and be that much more inclined to Like the page and to share updates from the page with others.

So follow the instructions in this lesson to get your page set up first, and then open the flood gates when you're positioned.

TIP: **Watching People Visit Your Page**

If you're really interested in what people think about your Facebook Page, have them visit it for the first time while you're with them. Watch where their eyes go and see what interests them and what doesn't. Ask them questions about what they like and don't like; assure them that you won't be offended by their opinion. Write down what you hear. This kind of input is invaluable in improving your page.

Why are Likes so important? A Like acts like a subscription to your status update; people who Like your page keep hearing from you, via your status update, while people who don't Like your page no longer hear from you. So you really want people who have a genuine interest in your business to take the step of clicking the Like button. (It's easy for them to stop receiving your updates later if they get tiresome.) So focus your early efforts on getting Likes.

Only you see the Get Started tab; users of your fan page don't see it. When in the infinite wisdom of Facebook's computers you've done enough to improve your page, the Get Started tab disappears.

Building Your Wall through Status Updates

An empty, blank wall is kind of boring, which has inspired generations of graffiti artists, going back even to Roman times and before. You don't want your Facebook Wall to be blank even when your earliest visitors come, let alone after your page has been up for a while. But what kind of content should you put on it?

Figure 8.1 shows the Wall for Transition San Francisco, a sustainability group with its own Facebook Page.

FIGURE 8.1   It's all just bricks in your Wall.

Text Status Updates

Status updates are usually most of what ends up populating your Wall. They're meant to be kind of offhand remarks sometimes, and important bits of news other times.

When something important happens, always enter a status update: a new employee starts or a current employee leaves; your holiday hours change; you get in a new item or offer a new service; and so on. Buffer the "newsy" updates with interesting ones about a customer encounter, an inspirational thought, or something funny an employee said.

The daily flow of news helps make your Facebook fans feel a part of your business and gently keeps you in their limited span of attention—so that, when they need to buy something you offer or to recommend someone to a friend, they think of you first. These little notes also serve as a valuable record of your daily activity.

There's another kind of status update, though, which is the more important kind for adding depth and personality to your Facebook presence. This kind of status update is more personal and interesting but shouldn't be too personal or too interesting. It's a balance. These kinds of updates should be easy to write, but sometimes getting them onto the screen can be quite a challenge.

Here are a few suggestions to help prevent writer's block when you're staring at those two little words on your fan page, "Write something":

- ▶ **What are you doing?** Make a note about what you're doing, even if it seems quite banal. "I just had the worst cup of coffee ever," can be pretty funny to someone who is sitting having a cup of coffee of his or her own. This immediacy is a core part of the appeal of Facebook, so use it on your Wall.

- ▶ **What just happened?** We all hear tons of news every day, but what are the things that are interesting and important to you? "I heard on the news today about the protests in Egypt," is mildly interesting; "I heard from my Mom in Cairo just now about the protests in Egypt," is compelling. This kind of update will reflect both your business and personal interests.

- ▶ **Tell me something great.** Share when something cool happens: "Best. Service. Ever. I just got my $20 back because the barber took off a little more than I had asked him to."

▶ **Tell me something awful.** "If you can't say anything nice about anyone, come sit by me," the saying goes. Don't insult anyone, but share something that really annoyed or irritated you.

▶ **What do you think?** Fish for comments without being heavy-handed about it. "What do you think?" "Has this ever happened to you?" "Share your best/worst customer service story." These kinds of prompts may help get interaction going.

NOTE: **We Interrupt Our Regular Program for an Update**

Consider scheduling your updates. You can actually create a calendar of Wall-worthy events and then fill in the spaces in between with ideas and random jottings. This will help you have something to say—and to keep saying something. Check your page at a regular time each workday and if you haven't yet posted anything, do so then. The start of the day is a good time to do this—that way, people get something from you to mull over or respond to during their workdays.

Photos on Your Wall

For many of your visitors, photos are the best way to make your site lively. Reactions vary—some people are very words-oriented and won't bother much with photos; others are image-oriented and will hardly stop to read your pearls of wisdom. So you have to have both in order to reach all of your audience. (Younger people tend to be very photo-oriented, and you won't reach most of them if you don't include images.)

A good way to think about words and pictures is that the words are the body of a cake, and the photos are the icing. To take the analogy even further, links are whipped cream, and video is the cherry on top!

The best way to get photos into the Photo tab is to add photo updates to your News Feed. That is, just keep taking photos relating to your business, then post them into your News Feed using the Photo link. (The four kinds of status update, shown at the top of your Wall, are Status, Photo, Link, and Video.) If you have a retail store, for instance, every new display or new item is worth a photo. You can do silly things like count people as they walk in or buy something, and then take a photo of your 100th customer of the week—or some similar fun update.

Link Updates

Web links are a really cool thing to share on Facebook. They're a way to deepen the discussion—or to add something fun or funny—without putting too much "stuff" into Facebook itself.

To add a link update to your Wall, follow these steps:

1. Find an interesting page on the Web; select the URL of the page from the top of the browser window, and copy it.

   Copy the URL of the specific page that you want to refer to, not the overall website address, such as www.nytimes.com, because you want to send someone directly to the page you're looking at.

2. On your Wall click the **Link** icon.

   The status entry update area changes to show the letters http:// and an **Attach** button.

3. Post the URL in the status entry update area.

   Part of the information from the web page shows up in the status entry area. In some cases, typically news stories, a photo will appear; and, in some of these cases, you can click arrows to move through a series of photos.

4. If there's an option, click the arrows to select the photo you want.

5. In the comment area, which has the words "Say something about this link," enter your comment.

   It's really important to enter a comment. People can find stories on the Web on their own; what they're interested in, when you post a story, is what you think about it.

6. Click the **Share** button.

The link is added to your News Feed, as shown in Figure 8.2, which also shows another Link update in progress. (In the figure, the link to the Transition Albany news has been entered, but it won't go out as a status update until the Share button is clicked.)

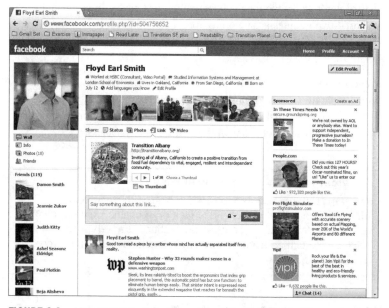

FIGURE 8.2   Link updates are a fun way to bring the Web to life among fans of your fan page.

When you do a link update, or any kind of status update for that matter, try to have some idea of what would be more appropriate for your business page than for your personal page. Over time, you'll develop a voice that's appropriate for your business and a different but complementary voice for yourself as an individual.

Video Updates

Sharing videos is just like sharing photos. You can upload them from your hard drive or record them directly with a webcam.

Using videos is really powerful because video is so evocative. Video tugs at the heartstrings for some messages; for others, it adds personality and richness that just aren't there with text or even with a photo.

Technical standards for video shared among friends on Facebook are very low, so don't worry too much about quality. Just have a little fun and keep it short—two minutes is an eternity for a Facebook video. Try for 30 seconds or so for most videos. (There's a reason 30 seconds is the standard length for a TV ad.)

Webcam videos are a bit more dubious for business use than videos shot with a separate camera. Young people love webcam videos, but the angle, lighting, and so on make most people look really awful. Experiment to find a way of using video that works well for your business.

> TIP: **Video Updates Without Video Files**
> You can do status updates to your fan page with video content without actually dealing with video files or webcams. Just do a link update, as described in the previous section, to a web page with a video on it, such as a YouTube video. This allows you to have more control over quality.

Updating the Info Tab

The Info area gets filled in when you set up your fan page, as described in the previous lesson. However, you should review the Info area for your fan page regularly. It looks really bad to go to the Info tab for a business and see obviously old, out-of-date information there.

For a retail store, for instance, it might be good to have an up-to-date list of salesclerks; for a law firm, of attorneys and others who interact with the public. Little, helpful, timely pieces of information like this make you appear thoughtful (because you are).

Also keep up the integration with your website; for instance, having a different company mission on Facebook versus what's on your company website might make people think that you're "mission" in action!

Managing the Photos Tab

The Photos tab has a record of all the photos you've uploaded as status updates. It also allows you to arrange photos that you've uploaded into albums. (Facebook does a certain amount of arranging itself, for instance putting every image that you've used as a profile picture in one album.)

It's great to arrange your photos in albums, but this isn't business-specific functionality, so I won't go into detail about it here. However, if you click the Account tab in the upper right corner of any Facebook Page and choose Help Center, which is shown in Figure 8.3, you can click Photos under Facebook Apps and Features to get information how to use photo albums.

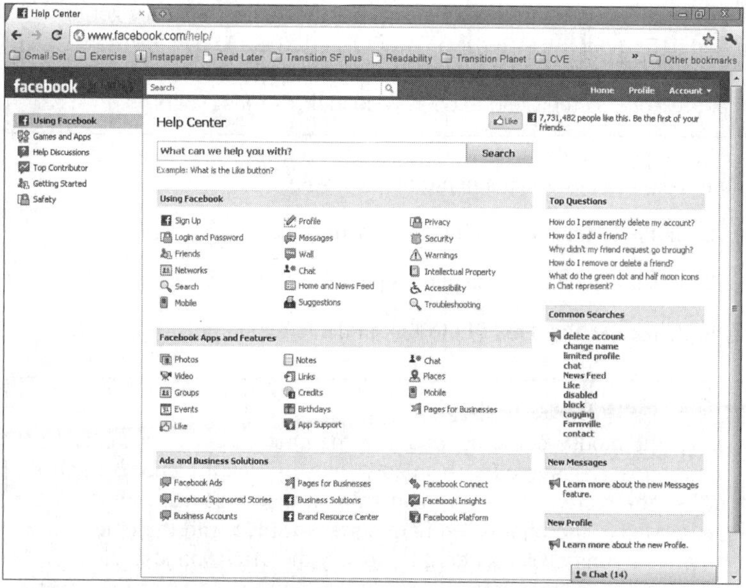

FIGURE 8.3 Facebook gives you help with photo albums—and much more.

When using Facebook, you might have noticed that some pictures are tagged with people's names. This is more important and valuable than you might think. When you tag a photo with the names of your Facebook friends, they're notified of it on Facebook, which is a very welcome and powerful way of keeping them in touch with you.

People tagged in photos on your Facebook Page may well share the photos further, which brings your business to the attention of their Facebook friends in a very positive way. The point isn't to manipulate the process, just to use Facebook's tools in a comfortable and natural way that will end up helping keep your business in the "mind's eye" of customers and their friends.

TIP: **Friend Before You Tag**

If there are people in a photo who are not yet your Facebook friends, consider sending out a friend request and waiting for the answer before you tag the photo. If the person or people in a photo are your Facebook friends, tagging them is easier, and they get notified in Facebook that they've been tagged. (People can link from their own profiles to photos they've been tagged in.) That way, the photo adds to their presence in Facebook, not just yours.

Follow these steps to tag a photo in Facebook:

1. In the left-hand rail, click the **Photos** link.

2. Click a photo, and the photo opens.

3. Click the **Tag This Photo** link in the left-hand rail.

NOTE: **More about Tagging**

When the mouse cursor is held over the photo, the cursor turns into a cross. This is odd, because when you click the photo, a sensitive little rectangular area—centered on the cross-hairs—is embedded in the photo. The name is associated with the little area. You don't click and drag to specify the area; you just click and release on the photo.

---

4. Click the center of a person's face or body. To move the box, click a different spot.

   A box appears with an area beneath it for text entry.

5. Click in the text entry area.

A list of recent tags appears, as shown in Figure 8.4.

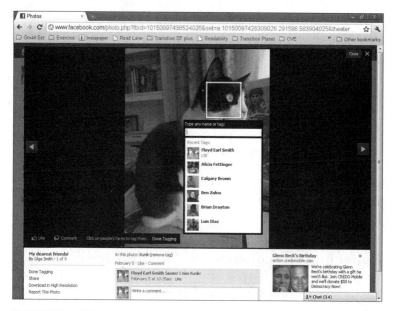

FIGURE 8.4   Click a person's face or body to tag them and then choose or enter a tag.

6. Choose a tag from the list or enter the name of a Facebook friend, and they'll appear in the drop-down list for you to choose; or enter a name or other tag that doesn't refer to a Facebook friend.

The tag appears in a list beneath the photo (as shown in Figure 8.4). To remove a tag, click the **Remove Tag** link.

7. Take other steps with the photo, such as adding a caption, adding a comment, sharing the photo, and so on.

Take your time and do all of these that make sense so the photo has the impact it should.

8. Click the **X** at upper right to finish with the photo.

Start Discussions

Discussions can be a great addition to your page. On some sites, though, discussion areas can be ghost towns—started with great hope, kept alive for a while with a few comments, then trailing off into stillness.

It's worth trying discussions to see if yours catch fire. If they do, there's hardly a better addition to your page. Discussions can be very engaging. They can also be helpful with practical matters such as customer support. More general discussions of the "Hi, how's it going," variety, however, have a varied track record for usefulness and longevity.

Customer support-type discussions have their own issues, though. People are usually quicker to complain than to give praise or thanks, so discussion boards can become pretty grim. Customer support discussions can conceivably discourage new customers from doing business with you, even if they're serving a valuable purpose in allowing existing customers to get difficult questions answered.

The possibility of a negative impression is not a reason not to try discussions, but it is a reason to monitor them closely. You'll need to encourage the kinds of comments that you want, take down comments that are not on target, and even consider closing the discussions if they go too far off into the weeds.

You'll have the best chance for success with your discussions if you start them at the beginning of your Facebook presence when your Facebook presence is fresh. That way, your early users—who may be among your most enthusiastic users—get a chance to be involved right from the start.

Follow these steps to start a discussion:

1. Click the **Discussions** tab.

   The Discussions page appears, which will be empty.

2. Click the **Start New Topic** button.

   Two text entry areas appear, Topic and Post, as shown in Figure 8.5.

3. Fill in the Topic and Post, then click the button, Post new topic.

   The new post is added, in a new topic.

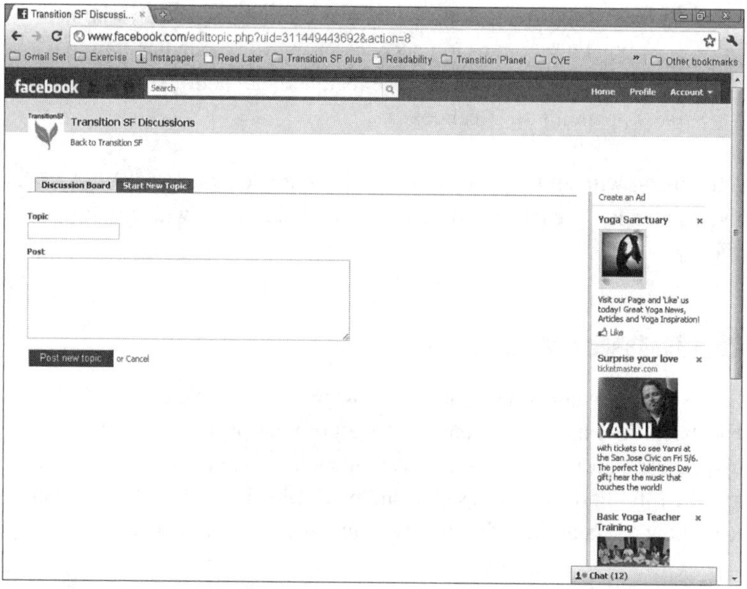

FIGURE 8.5 A chance to comment—or to suffer from writer's block.

Add Links, Notes, Videos, and Events

There are additional tabs that you can add to your Facebook Page quite easily: Links, Notes, Videos, and Events. These additional tabs are represented by a + symbol, which you have to click to view.

To add any of these tabs, just click the + button in the page setup area. Choose the area:

▶ **Links.** Links are just a record of Link postings you've made to your Wall, as described earlier in this lesson.

▶ **Notes.** Notes are a record of Notes postings, which are used rather rarely, in my experience.

▶ **Videos.** The Videos page is like the Photos page, allowing people to see videos you've posted and arranged into albums.

▶ **Events.** This area is not used by many people, but those who use it well get a lot out of it. Facebook events are a popular way to arrange things, and you can use regular email addresses for people who aren't on Facebook.

Experiment with all these areas. They can be tremendously useful. And the Events area is a great tool, especially if you hold events with any frequency at all.

Summary

In this lesson, you learned when and how to invite people to your Facebook Page and how to build the Wall of your page through status updates using text, photos, links, and video. You also learned how to manage the Info, Photos, Discussions, and other tabs. In the next lesson, you'll learn how to claim, modify, and use your Facebook Places page.

LESSON 9

Claiming Your Places Page

In this lesson, you learn how Facebook Places coordinates with your Facebook Page and how to add (if necessary), edit, and claim your Places page. You also learn how to combine your Facebook Page and your Places page—and why that often isn't a good idea.

Understanding How Places Fits In

Facebook Places is designed to meet many of the same needs as Google Places, which came out earlier. A Facebook Place is a page on Facebook tied to a specific location, usually of a business or other entity. The idea of both Google Places and Facebook Places is to provide a kind of online Yellow Pages entry with key information about places and a target for mapping to help you get there, call, or otherwise be in touch.

Facebook Places is less structured than Google Places, and Facebook Places can include people's homes. The information included in Facebook Places is very simple: the location (shown on a map), the name, and a description. An example of a Facebook Place is shown in Figure 9.1, captured from an iPad. Note that the Place includes a Deal for $25 with a styling session. ("Bart" refers to the Bay Area Rapid Transit system, which is an urban train system like the New York subway, London Underground, and so on.)

The genius part of Facebook Places is the idea that anyone visiting a real place can "check in" to the Facebook Place that matches it. Facebook interaction usually takes your real-world ties—friendships, family relationships, romantic relationships—and gives them a home online. Facebook Places takes your online Facebook world and brings it back into the here

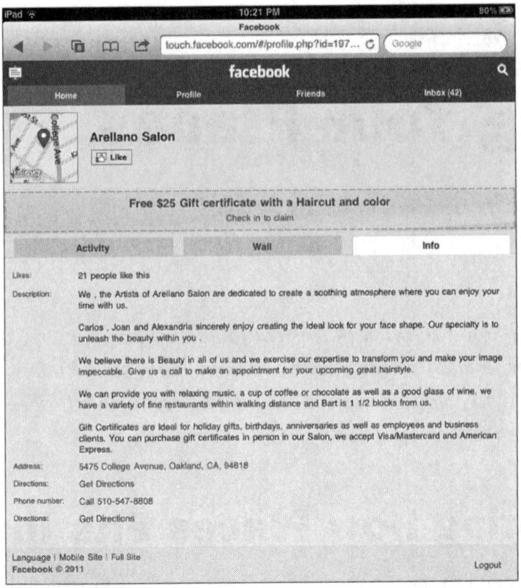

FIGURE 9.1   Facebook Places are very simple, indeed.

and now. You can even see other Facebook Places users who have "checked in" to the same location as you, even if you're not Facebook Friends or otherwise connected.

From a business point of view, though, Facebook created a bit of a monster with Facebook Places. Anyone can create a Place for a business whether he owns or works for the business or not. And he can write anything in the business description that he darn well pleases, misspell your business name, put you in the wrong location, and so on. (All this is true of Google Places as well.)

To get back control, you have to claim the Place and prove you're the business owner. Once you do that, no one else can change it. This lesson describes how to claim your page.

Once you've claimed your Facebook Place and perhaps cleaned it up a bit, you can start encouraging people to use it. There are several reasons you, and they, might want to check in:

▶ **To see where their friends have been.** When people use Facebook Places to check in, they see a list of places that their friends have "checked in" to recently. An example, captured from an iPad, is shown in Figure 9.2. You want your business to be on that list, prompting people to come to your business because their friends have been there.

FIGURE 9.2   Facebook shows people where their friends have checked in recently.

▶ **To see who's here now.** Facebook shows people who check in the names of other Facebook users who recently checked in to the same place. Not only their friends—just other Facebook users. So if someone comes up to you in the refreshments line at the movie theatre and says, "Hello—are you on Facebook?" they haven't lost their minds; they've seen your check-in on Facebook Places.

▶ **To get Facebook Deals.** When you check in to a Place, you get to see any Facebook Deals that the business offers customers who check in. Right now, Facebook Deals isn't used widely enough to make it worth checking in just to see Facebook Deals.

At some point, though, Facebook will promote this effectively, and it may well become common practice. You can jump-start the process for your own business by creating Facebook Deals and then advertising them in your business as described in Lesson 10, "Creating Facebook Deals."

Facebook promotes the creation of something called the "social graph" for each of its users—an online representation within Facebook of the people and, yes, places you interact with in your life. You can see how Facebook Places plays a crucial role in deepening the social graph by encouraging you to visit places your friends visit, to make new friends from among Facebook users who are at the same place you are, and to deepen your in-person business relationships by encouraging you to check in and get Facebook-only offers.

This process—of tying in your business to people's journeys and relation-ships—is what you seek to become part of by creating a Facebook Page, by claiming your Places page, and by offering Facebook Deals and adver-tising on Facebook.

> NOTE: **What If You Are No Place?**
> Facebook fan pages make a great deal of sense for small, virtual businesses that don't have physical offices or other locations for people to visit. But how about Facebook Places for this sort of business? You can just skip the whole thing, or you can take a tongue-in-cheek approach—creating a Places page, for instance, that has its physical location in the nearby coffee shop where you hang out and have casual business meetings. Have fun with it—but be cautious before putting your home address on Facebook if you don't otherwise share it widely.

Understanding How to Claim Your Place

Anyone can create a Facebook Place. This section gives you an overview of the process; a section later in the lesson, "Adding Your Place," tells you exactly how to do it.

Let's say you go to your local movie theater and want to check in to let people know you're there. If a Facebook Place already exists for the theater, you see the Place when you go to check in; if there isn't a Facebook Place for the theater, though, you can quickly create one.

The problem is that the details that an ordinary customer enters—the specific name of the theater, the description, even the exact location that Facebook gives the theater—might not be correct, or at least might not be exactly how the owner would like the business's references to look.

So, as the owner or manager of a business, you need to take control of the Facebook Place description for your business. You do this by claiming the place and verifying that you are indeed the owner, as mentioned earlier.

This process can be a hassle for small businesses that aren't listed in the phone book—Facebook uses your business phone number as the easiest way to verify ownership—but it's worth doing. Facebook marketing is only going to become more important over time; the sooner you claim your Facebook Place, the sooner you can start doing a better job with it.

The overall process goes like this:

▶ On the Facebook website (not the mobile version or an app), check to see if your business already exists as a Facebook Place. Use Facebook's search functionality to look for your business name.

▶ If your business exists as a Facebook Place, claim the Place; if not, go to your business location, if you're not there already, and use a mobile device and an app—or the mobile Facebook site—to add your business as a Place to Facebook Places.

▶ In Facebook (not the mobile version or an app), claim the Place as your own. Edit it if needed.

The steps to achieve all this are described in the remaining sections in this lesson.

NOTE: What If You Have Multiple Locations?

If you have multiple locations, create a separate Facebook Place for each of them. You will not be able to merge all these separate

Facebook Places with your overall Facebook Page for your business, as businesses with just one location are able to do. In my view, this is not a bad thing.

Adding Your Place

Before you can claim your Place, you or someone else has to add it to Facebook.

NOTE: **Adding Your Place, Your Way**

Because anyone can add a Places page, the same real-world place can be added several times as different Places pages. Each could have a slightly different version of the name, different descriptions, and so on. So if your business has already been added as a Place, I suggest you go ahead and add it yourself anyway. That way, you can use the exact spelling, capitalization, and so on of the name that you want, and the specific description that you want. Then once you have the Places page in, well...place...get people to Like it. When "your" Places page is the most-Liked, it will rise to the top of the list when people search for it on Facebook or through Facebook Places. And with placement at the top of the list, it will get more Likes and attention.

Follow these steps to add your Facebook Place (you learn how to claim it in the next section):

1. Search for your business using the Search bar on Facebook. If you find your Places page, skip to the next section; otherwise, create a Places page for your business using these steps.

   In my experience, Facebook search is not very good, and when you search from within the main Facebook site, there's no geographical limit on the search. As a result, you might have trouble finding your business if some or all of the words involved are common. Also, your business might exist as a Place, but with the name misspelled, or it could exist several times under the same name or variations. See Figure 9.3 for an example search with multiple results.

FIGURE 9.3   CineArts has lots of Places pages (with the pushbutton icon) and other search results as well.

2. Get the necessities together for checking in to a Facebook Place. That is, get a smartphone with a Facebook app that supports Places, such as the iPhone Facebook app or the Facebook Places check-in app for Android phones. If you don't have an app—or if you're using a tablet such as the iPad or Android tablets—load up the website, touch.facebook.com, into your browser.

3. Go—that is, physically travel to, not "go" on the Web—to the store, office, taco shop, or other kind of business that you want to create a Facebook Place for.

Go to the exact location—not, say, a coffee shop nearby— because you will want the right location to be stored in Facebook to be used by people trying to visit you.

4. Using your mobile phone, tablet computer, or other device that supports Facebook check-ins, go to Facebook Places.

An example of using Facebook Places on the iPad, using the touch.facebook.com site, was shown in Figures 9.1 and 9.2.

> **NOTE: For More on Using the iPad**
>
> For more about the iPad, see my books: *Sams Teach Yourself iPad in 10 Minutes* (1st and 2nd editions) and *Using the Apple iPad*; the latter has online audio files and video clips.

5. Try to check in to your business. Begin by clicking the **Share where you are with friends** link.

   An Add button, a search box, and a list of places that you have previously checked in to appears.

6. Start typing the name of your business.

   Facebook will look for matches as you type. It will only look among places in your immediate vicinity.

   If no match appears, add your Place, as described in the next step. If a match appears, and you're happy with the details shown, you're done with adding your Place (as it's already there, and accurate).

7. If no match appears, press Add.

   The Add a Place dialog appears, as shown in Figure 9.4. The dialog doesn't show the name you had searched for, but it does show a map with your current location—the location that the Place will be assigned to. Check the map for accuracy before proceeding.

8. Fill in the Name field for your business and, optionally, the Description field.

   The name is required—each Place in Facebook is a combination of a location and a name. Adding a description is optional but highly recommended. You can enter anything here, but a short, catchy description of your business, plus a phone number, might do the trick. You might want to include your business hours as well.

FIGURE 9.4 You might get to create your own Place.

9. Tap the **Add** button.

Your Place appears onscreen, inviting you to check in.

10. Tap the **Like** button so you're subscribed for updates. If you have Facebook friends with you, get their permission and then tap the **Tag Friends With You** link and enter their names. Then enter a brief comment and tap the **Check In** button to, well, check in.

Your check-in shows up in the Activity tab.

11. Tap the **Info** tab to check the information you entered, the directions link, and so on.

The Info tab was shown previously in Figure 9.1.

Editing Your Place

You can go in and edit or delete a Place you've created. Just go to the Places page on the Web—not on a mobile device—and look for the **Edit Page** link in the upper-right corner. Click the link, and you'll be able to change the name and description. You can also delete the Place.

Unfortunately, this ability to edit the Places page only lasts for a limited time; Facebook doesn't say exactly how long. I'd guess that you can count on being able to make a change the next day, but perhaps not the next week.

The fact that your Places page becomes uneditable limits its uses. For instance, you can't put in your business hours if there's any chance they'll ever change. (Even if your basic hours stay the same, you'd want to be able to change them around the holidays.)

In fact, it's actually unacceptable that you can't keep editing your Places page. The purpose of your business or the way in which you want to describe it can certainly change over time. You need to be able to change your Places page to match. Unfortunately, though, you can't.

We can assume that Facebook will change this eventually as the number of Places with outdated information becomes a problem. But when they might make such a change, and exactly what form it might take, is impossible to guess.

Claiming Your Place

If your business phone number is in a phone book or otherwise available, Facebook might call you at that number as its main verification method to allow you to claim your Places page. So be near that phone for this process if possible. Alternatively, Facebook may ask for a business email address (with a recognizable domain name), or a scanned or photographed copy of a utility bill with the correct information on it. You might want to be ready with one of these, if you have them.

When you know your Place is on Facebook—either because you found it already there, or added it yourself—it's time to claim it as your own. Follow these steps:

1. Find your business using the Search bar on Facebook. (This has to be from the full Facebook site, not from a mobile device.)

Your Places page appears. (Facebook doesn't know that it's "yours" yet, but Facebook doesn't much care who created a Places page, just who claims it.) Figure 9.5 is an example of a Places page.

FIGURE 9.5   Your Places page asks if this is your business.

2. Click the **Is this your business?** link.

   A verification window appears, as shown in Figure 9.6.

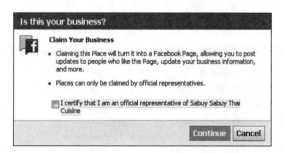

FIGURE 9.6   Facebook asks you to verify that you're an official representative of the business.

3. Click the checkbox to certify that you're an official representative of the business. Click the **Continue** button.

Any of several things might now happen, depending on what method Facebook chooses to use to verify your business. If Facebook can find a listed phone number for your business, it will verify you by phone. You'll see a dialog box like the one in Figure 9.7; follow the onscreen instructions to complete the verification process.

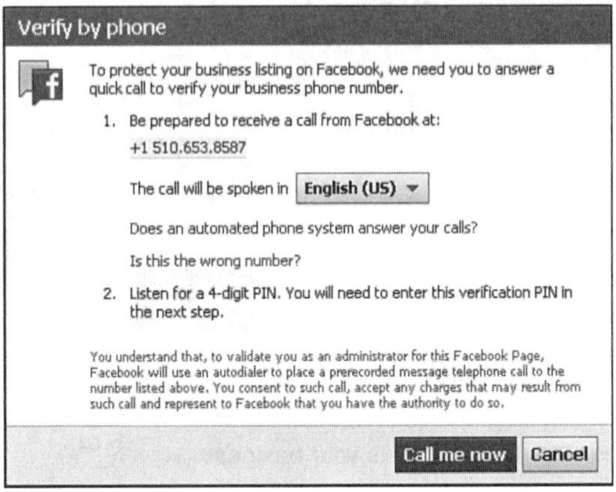

Verify by phone

To protect your business listing on Facebook, we need you to answer a quick call to verify your business phone number.

1. Be prepared to receive a call from Facebook at:

   +1 510.653.8587

   The call will be spoken in [English (US) ▼]

   Does an automated phone system answer your calls?

   Is this the wrong number?

2. Listen for a 4-digit PIN. You will need to enter this verification PIN in the next step.

You understand that, to validate you as an administrator for this Facebook Page, Facebook will use an autodialer to place a prerecorded message telephone call to the number listed above. You consent to such call, accept any charges that may result from such call and represent to Facebook that you have the authority to do so.

[Call me now] [Cancel]

FIGURE 9.7 Facebook might be able to verify you with a phone call.

If Facebook can't find a listed phone number, you get a more complex verification page like the one shown in Figure 9.8.

4. Fill out all the information carefully. Choose an authentication method and follow the instructions onscreen.

Note carefully the warning at the bottom of the screen verifying that you are authorized to act on behalf of the business. Facebook can suspend users who make false or unfounded claims, and getting such suspensions reversed is difficult. So only follow these steps if you're the legitimate representative of the business.

5. Click **Submit**.

Your request will be submitted. You might get a quick phone call and be approved on the spot, or it could take several days for Facebook to review your submission and decide whether to assign the page to you.

FIGURE 9.8 Facebook has a multiple-choice verification process.

Combining Places and Pages

After you've verified ownership of your Place, Facebook offers you the option of merging your Places page and your fan page for your business.

I suggest you *not* merge the pages—and there are lots of opinions in various blogs and online forums about Facebook to back me up. Here are seven reasons why you should not merge your Places page and the fan page for your business:

▶ **The merged page looks too much like a "normal" Facebook page.** Facebook Places are very "light," with just a name and description. They actually should be bulked up a bit to include business hours and so on—like a Google Place. But the merged page is too much, not something someone wants to try to navigate around on her iPhone while trying to come visit your location. Given the different devices people use and the way they use them, you're probably better off with separate pages than a merged one.

▶ **Merged pages can't handle multiple locations.** A merged page only works with one location. If you have multiple locations, you only get one on the merged page; the rest just disappear from Facebook. This is confusing for customers and could even cost you business.

▶ **The merged page is not like the big guys.** The big brands have multiple locations, so they don't merge their pages. And it's the big brands that Facebook users go to the most. If you have a merged page, it will be different from what people have gotten used to, and different from the big brand names that they're familiar with.

▶ **Merging is problematic.** Some businesses add customer features to their Facebook Pages, such as custom coding, coupons, and so on. This custom code tends to disappear during a merge and has to be re-created on the merged page.

▶ **Unmerging is problematic.** In response to complaints, Facebook now offers a way to unmerge pages back into a Places page and a Facebook Page for your business. However, the unmerged pages have been reported to have problems, such as loss of data from the pre-merged Facebook Page, and even bugs that make the unmerged pages harder to find in Facebook.

▶ **Support is poor.** Facebook has a poor reputation for support. They're generally responsive on a lot of big and even medium-sized issues, steadily improving their offering in response to comments, questions, and complaints. But actual support—getting a specific answer to your question, getting help recovering data from a deleted account, and so on—is said to be poor. So it's best to avoid potential problems, because you might not get much help fixing them.

There are a few advantages to having a merged page, however. It's only one thing for you to manage and for the user to have to deal with. If you're going to keep your Facebook Page for your business very simple anyway, and if you're sure you won't have multiple locations anytime soon, you might prefer the simplicity of the merged page. For most businesses, though, I recommend avoiding the merge.

> **NOTE: Managing Multiple Locations**
>
> If you have multiple locations, create a Facebook Page for the entire business and separate Places pages for each location. Give each location a specific and consistent name, such as BigChain Pizza—Carney St. This allows people to find and check in to the specific location.

Summary

In this lesson, you learned how Facebook Places fits with your Facebook Page and how to add (if necessary), edit, and claim your Places page. You also learned how to combine your Facebook Page and your Places page—and why that often isn't a good idea. In the next lesson, you learn how to create Facebook Deals.

LESSON 10

Creating Facebook Deals

In this lesson, you learn the advantages of Facebook Deals and how to see whether or not you can offer them. You then learn what the elements of a Deal are, how to craft them, and how to create a Deal.

Understanding the Advantages of Facebook Deals

Facebook Deals have a lot of potential to make a difference in your business. And for most businesses that get the opportunity, it's well worth it to start using Facebook Deals now while it's still the "early" days.

Facebook Deals are likely to become more and more important in the years to come. You and other businesspeople you know may very well use Deals as a regular part of their businesses—especially because, at this writing, Deals are free.

You see, Facebook Deals encourage engagement with Facebook when people are out and about—something that Facebook is eager to promote. And they encourage business owners and managers—that's you—to not only create Deals, which are free, but to buy Facebook Ads to promote them, which is not. (Facebook Ads are described in the next lesson.)

So why is it especially important to get started with Deals right away? As mentioned earlier, the first reason is that they're free at this writing, so the only investment is your time and effort. (Which, of course, are likely to be in short supply.) That might not last forever though, so it's good to get through the learning curve now.

Also, the early days of Facebook Deals are a bit like the early days of radio or TV advertising. People still talk about a Southern California car dealer named Cal Worthington who's been creating TV ads for years. His ads would show him strolling across his car sales lot saying, "I'm Cal Worthington, and this is my dog Spot." The "dog," of course, was a tiger, or a grizzly bear, or an elephant—anything except an actual dog.

You can see Cal Worthington's ads—and perhaps get a little inspiration for your own advertising, including Facebook Deals—at www.mydogspot. com. See Figure 10.1 for an example of a typical Cal Worthington ad.

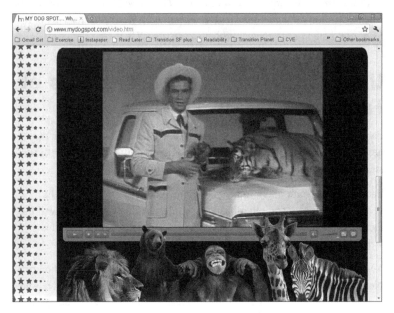

FIGURE 10.1   Visit www.mydogspot.com to see Cal Worthington selling cars.

With Facebook Deals, as with early TV ads, you have a chance to use new technology to make a strong, favorable impression with your customers. The new technologies are smartphones, which are growing very quickly; Facebook, which is growing very quickly; and Facebook Deals, which is also likely to grow very quickly.

Out of Facebook's 500 million-plus users, more than 200 million already use Facebook on their smartphones. "Checking in" to places is just getting started, but is likely to become very popular—especially if Deals become popular. Figure 10.2 shows a Deal on an iPhone, still the most popular single type of smartphone today. (Android phones, as a group, are now outselling the iPhone.)

FIGURE 10.2   An ad agency gives donuts away to visitors for fun.

Deals don't just make the Facebook user who claims the Deal feel good; when a user claims a Deal, an update goes out to every one of that user's Facebook friends, as shown in Figure 10.3. That could be hundreds of people, most of whom probably live or work near your business. This is very valuable free advertising for you.

This lesson explains who can and can't offer Facebook Deals and tells you how to set them up. Lesson 12, "Pricing and Creating Your Ad Campaign," tells you how to promote your whole Facebook presence, including Deals.

FIGURE 10.3   All Kelli's Friends know she claimed a Deal.

I'm suggesting here, though, that you start thinking now about putting a lot of effort behind Facebook Deals (if, that is, you can offer them; see the next section). Really good advertising gets people talking, and it's easy to use Facebook Deals to get people talking.

Just offer creative, interesting, highly rewarding, even—occasionally—outrageous Deals. Figure out what your equivalent of "my dog Spot" is, and use that in your Deals and other ads and publicity. Publicize Deals through status updates, through signs at your location, and by talking to customers about them.

You don't have to spend a lot of money either. Using Facebook Deals to give out ten free car washes might cost you a hundred dollars. (You can offer free car washes whether your business is a car wash or not. You can even wash the cars yourself!) For that hundred dollars, or less if you provide free labor, you're likely to get a whole bunch of people talking.

People want to do cool things with their smartphones. They want to do cool things with Facebook. People use both their smartphones and

Facebook to stay in touch with friends and family. So if you create a cool Deal that shows up via Facebook on someone's smartphone while she's in your shop, she's very much inclined to share it with the people she cares about.

And you don't have to be the first one in the world, or even in your country, to do something interesting with Deals in order to make a splash. Facebook Deals are local-focused, so you just have to be the first one on your block. Yes, Starbucks and others have already beaten you to the punch by using Deals to make an offer—a weak one, just 10% off. But big companies tend to be boring and conservative. You have the opportunity to offer a Deal that really gets people talking.

Finding Out If You Can Offer Facebook Deals

Not every business can offer Facebook Deals. Facebook reviews your Facebook Page, and perhaps other sources of information, before allowing you to offer Facebook Deals.

So how do you know if you can offer Facebook Deals? Simple—just look on your Places page after you claim it. If there's a green button that says Create a Deal, you can offer Facebook Deals. If there's no button, unfortunately, you can't.

There are no published criteria, and there's no appeals process. One would hope that the ability to offer Facebook Deals will rapidly be rolled out to anyone who claims a Places page, but there's no way of knowing if that will turn out to be the case.

CAUTION: **Keeping It Real**

Facebook can reject your Deal if it's seen as frivolous or low quality. This is to keep quality up, so that Facebook users keep seeing Facebook Deals as worthwhile. You should have the same concern where it relates to your own business and its image. Make your Deals strong enough that people get excited about them, and you should be fine.

It does make some sense that Facebook would limit this capability initially. When you create a Facebook Deal, you have to send it in to Facebook for review. Facebook promises a response within about two days. At some point, a human has to review the ad and probably offer an explanation if it's being turned down. Facebook might even have to engage in some back and forth with you around what changes it wants to make an ad acceptable.

When Apple opened the App Store for the iPhone, it went through a lot of growing pains with getting app reviewers trained, describing its rules to people, being consistent, and so on. Facebook needs to be sure it can handle the number of Deals coming through for review and try to keep the number of shady Deals to a minimum. However, those of us who use Facebook deserve some transparency from the company on the standards it's currently using, and where it's going with the process in the future.

> NOTE: **Making Your Own Deals**
>
> If Facebook isn't letting you offer Deals—or if you are allowed to offer Facebook Deals but don't have time to wait a couple of days for the reviewing process—you can accomplish the same thing on your own. Just use the same publicity as you would for a Facebook Deal and give the offer to anyone who comes to your location(s) and shows you that they've checked in to your Facebook Places page. You can then make further offers to people who are Facebook friends of people who've checked in previously. This approach might even be more fun and just as effective as the standardized Facebook Deals.

Thinking Up Deals

It's worth giving some thought to Facebook Deals before you create your first one. Here are some typical types of deals—you can use these as models or as inspiration for wilder and crazier ideas of your own:

▶ **Discounts.** Giving money off—10% off, 20% off, $5 off—is the most proven way of getting people in the door. You're trying to generate "buzz," so consider making some crazy offers in the

mix, or surprise people by giving them something free, along
with more typical discounts.

▶ **Two-for-one offers, three-for-two offers, and so on.** Free items
for multiple-item purchases are very attractive to customers, giving that "something for nothing" feeling that encourages impulse
buying.

▶ **Free support, free service.** Giving free service or free support is
often a good way to get some "buzz" out of something that
doesn't cost you that much to offer.

▶ **Free initial consultation.** It's often in your interest to give a free
initial consultation to jump-start a purchasing process. Making
the initial consultation free can work well for you as well as your
customers.

▶ **Charitable contributions.** Facebook Deals make it easy to give
a donation to charity with a purchase, as described later in this
lesson. This is a great incentive for people. You can also combine
charity with a discount to encourage "doing well while doing
good."

You can get further ideas by paying attention to ads you encounter in daily
life. Coupon books and newspapers are good sources for Deals ideas.

Facebook itself is using spectacular offers as it rolls out its own Deals.
During a European launch in January 2011, Facebook offered a 20% discount—not usually a show-stopper. But the 20% discount was on a Mazda
MX sports car! The deal was really popular. The total cost of the promotion was more than half a million dollars, but it got lots of attention for
both Facebook and Mazda.

To help launch their use of Facebook places, Gap clothing stores gave the
first 10,000 people to check in to a Gap store a free pair of jeans. The
University of Kentucky encourages students to check in around campus,
promoting the school to their friends (not a Deal, strictly speaking, but
clever marketing). And the Palms Hotel and Casino offered a free night or
a room upgrade to customers who check in on Facebook. Check-ins
increased by a factor of four.

> TIP: **Free and New, New and Free**
>
> There are two words that are said to get people's attention most strongly in marketing: "free" and "new." So if you can work "free" (or a discount) and "new" (or updated, improved, and so on) into your ads, you're more likely to have a winner.

All these offers are conventional, "one-to-one" deals, meaning your business is giving a benefit directly to a customer. The real magic of any kind of advertising on Facebook comes when you can use your advertising and Facebook to move along the "social graph," the web of a person's real-world relationships.

An example of a social graph is shown in Figure 10.4. This example is from TouchGraph, a product that maps people's social networks. You can try the TouchGraph app on Facebook to map your own social world.

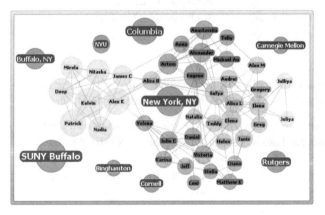

FIGURE 10.4   TouchGraph shows people's connections.

Think of how to involve people's Facebook friends in your Deals. Here are some ideas to get you started:

▶ **Give discounts to groups.** You can offer a Facebook Deal if three or more people come in together, for instance, or offer an increased discount for larger groups. This gets bodies into your store and hopefully expands your customer base. It also gets groups of friends and family members talking about you.

▶ **Give out paper coupons.** When someone comes in to claim a Facebook Deal, give him a paper coupon or some kind of fun item, like a toy flashlight. The recipient can keep the item or give it to a friend. The coupon or item is then worth a discount when someone brings it in.

▶ **Give out referral bonuses.** Ask people who take advantage of your Deals who referred them. Give the customer in front of you a coupon with the referrer's name on it. When the referrer comes in, he or she gets a special discount. (This might even be a good time to give something away for free.)

▶ **Use time limits and drawings.** People respond to urgency, and they love a chance at a big prize. Use deadlines, offer entries in a raffle, and give prizes to groups.

Every business is different. Some products and services have niche appeal—very few people are model railroad hobbyists, for instance, but the ones in your area may well know each other—so you can target deals to getting members of this informal network involved. Some products and services are generic, so much of the competition is on price, ease of buying, free delivery, and so on.

Figure out whether your customers are tied to each other and use that information to create Deals—and other offers outside of Facebook—that get friends to recommend you to their friends.

NOTE: **Having a Theme to Your Deals**

Your customers' heads are filled with information about hundreds of businesses they interact with. To stand out in their minds, be consistent in your Deals and in all you do. For instance, pick a single cause or charity and mention it repeatedly on your website, your Facebook Page, and in Charity Deals. If you do this right, when people hear your business mentioned, they'll think of your cause as well—and when they hear the cause mentioned, they'll remember that you're a supporter of it.

Creating a Deal

You can and should plan your Deals before you create them. Because the approval process takes a couple of days, you want to get the details right before you apply.

Here are the things you need to decide:

► **Type of Deal.** You can create an Individual Deal—the simplest kind; a Friend Deal, for groups that come in together; a Loyalty Deal, which kicks in after some number of visits; and a Charity Deal, which gives money to a charity when people check in (not when they check in and also buy, which some of us might have preferred).

► **Your offer.** Sum up the deal in a few words, such as "Free pair of tennis shoes with dress shoes." Sum up how to claim it in a few words as well: "Present this coupon at purchase."

► **Start and end dates.** When will the offer start and end? Give the dates and times.

► **Quantity.** You can stop showing a Deal after it's been claimed a certain number of times, which is a great fail-safe if a Deal proves really popular.

► **Repeatability.** You can limit a deal to one claim per Facebook user—or let a user claim the same deal once a day for the duration of the offer.

CAUTION: **Edit Your Work Carefully**

Editing your text carefully is crucial for something like a Facebook Deal. You'll only be entering perhaps a dozen words total—the offer and how to claim it. But any typos in those few words will reflect badly on you and your business. After you've entered all the fields for a deal, capture a screenshot before you press the Create Deal button. (Press Alt+PrtScr to capture the active window; then press Ctrl+V to paste the image into an email or word processing document.) Email the deal to some people and print out a copy so you—and perhaps a trusted friend or two—can review it on paper. Make any changes you need—then repeat the process every time you make a change until you're sure it's write. (Did you catch that one?)

Once you've figured all this out, dive in! Here's how to create a Deal:

1. Search for your business using the Search bar on Facebook. Find your Places page and look for the green **Create a Deal** button.

   If there's no button, you're not eligible to create Deals at this time. Hopefully Facebook will increase the number of businesses that can offer Deals over time.

2. When you click the **Create a Deal** button, the Create a Deal page appears, as shown in Figure 10.5.

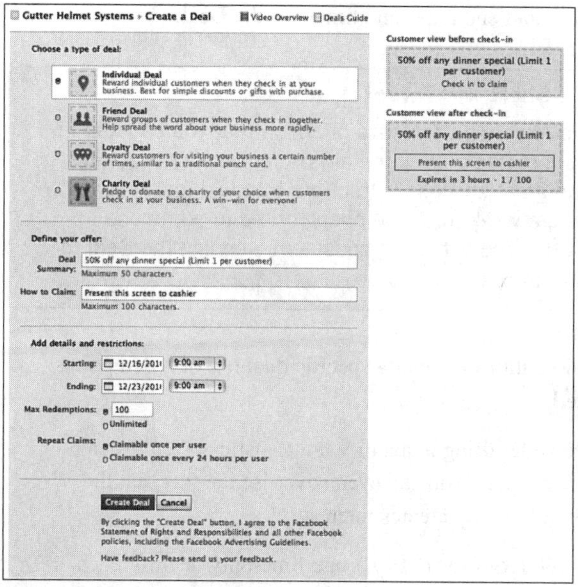

FIGURE 10.5 Creating a Deal is easy and fun.

3. Click a radio button to select the type of deal.

The options are Individual Deal, for when users check in alone; Friend Deal, for when they check in as a group; Loyalty Deal, to reward an individual visiting several times; or Charity Deal, to make a donation when a person checks in.

4. Enter the text for the offer.

"Three scoops for the price of two." "20% discount on your order." "Free alterations with new jeans." Use the shortest form of words that will make sense in the context of your business.

5. Describe how to claim the offer.

When the customer checks in, words will appear on the Deal about how to claim it. A simple description such as "Present at check-out counter" will do it.

6. Enter the start and end dates and times for the Deal.

TIP: **Keep Deals Short and Sweet**

Urgency is one of the biggest drivers of action that you can use in marketing—so short Deals are generally preferred over long ones. Groupon has had great success with offers that last just one day; for your business, a week might be enough time for someone to hear about the offer and act. (Also consider extending the Deal for a couple of days at the end.)

---

7. Use the radio buttons to enter a specific quantity of redemptions or **Unlimited**.

Seriously consider using a quantity limit, just in case the deal proves "too" popular. You can even advertise the fact that the deal is limited; scarcity creates interest.

8. Use the radio buttons to specify a one-time-only deal for each user or a deal that can be claimed once every day the offer is active.

Because Facebook Deals are just getting going, letting your early adopters use a deal multiple times might be attractive.

9. Click the **Create Deal** button.

The deal goes out for review. You'll receive an email update when it goes live. You can use the time to promote the deal, as described in Lesson 12.

Summary

In this lesson, you learned the advantages of Facebook Deals and how to see whether you can offer them. You then learned what the elements of a Deal are, how to craft them, and how to create a Deal. In the next lesson, you begin learning about Facebook Ads, starting with how to plan and target them.

Planning and Targeting Facebook Ads

In this lesson, you learn the method and considerations for planning your advertisements. This includes how to budget for your Facebook Ads, how to target your Ads to avoid "wastage," and how to design your Ad.

Budgeting for Your Ad Campaign

Facebook is the most promising new advertising platform around. With Facebook's fast growth and innovative ways of tying people together, there's great opportunity for successful advertising—and a lot of the best things you can do are free. Even Facebook Deals are free to run on Facebook, although of course there's a cost inherent in whatever offer you make.

Facebook Ads, though, are formal advertising: You create an Ad, specify where and when you want it to run, and then pay Facebook for running it.

You can view Facebook Ads as the cherry on your Facebook marketing and advertising sundae. The cherry is "eye candy"—it gets attention and gets people to engage. However, the whole package—the cherry, the ice cream, and the toppings—all have to look good and work well together for the whole effort to be worthwhile.

To make effective use of Facebook Ads, you need to understand something about the way Facebook allows you to target Ads. The more effective your targeting, the more likely it is that you can create a profitable campaign.

Facebook Ads are the only tool described in this book that costs you money directly—and it's very direct indeed. You commit to a daily budget for your Ads; Facebook then runs the Ads up to that limit, day after day, and charges you the agreed-on amount each day.

It's hard to generalize, but you may well end up paying about $1 for every click a Facebook user makes on your Ad. So to get ten clicks—enough, in many cases, to expect one sale as a result—you need to commit $10 a day, or about $300 a month. In this scenario, each sale is costing you $10. If you find the Ads to be effective, you might then double your budget. That's a big commitment for most small businesses.

NOTE: **Think Profit, Not Revenue**

When you spend $500 on advertising, you have to make $500 in sales to pay for it, right? Well, that's actually a way for you to go broke in a hurry. You actually need to make $500 in profit, after taxes, to pay for $500 in advertising. Depending on your business, that might mean making $2,000 to $3,000 worth of sales to break even on every $500 you spend on advertising. Now if you attract and keep customers, you can think of the long-term value of their business, not just the first visit. However, any way you slice it, you still have to make thousands of dollars in revenue to pay yourself back for spending $500 on advertising.

These budget amounts are not set in stone. But if you spend much less than a few hundred dollars a month, you probably won't get much in the way of results. Given that you're going to be spending a fair amount of time planning, creating, and managing your Ads, you should plan to spend enough to make some sales as a reward for your effort. So this kind of budget is sensible. You can set a much smaller budget while experimenting, but eventually you'll probably need to commit to some serious expenditures.

How can this kind of spending be worth it? Think of Facebook advertising as the visible tip of your Facebook presence. If you're spending thousands of dollars worth of your or your employees' time on your Facebook presence, you probably want the incisive effect of Facebook Ads to help bring people to it.

Facebook Ads can be very good at bringing in not just people, but strong Facebook networkers, to your business. In the famous book, *The Tipping*

Point, by Malcolm Gladwell, such people are called connectors. Gladwell says that your goal is to start an "epidemic" of interest in your business—with buying from you as the cure! A graphic showing some of the factors involved in creating such an outbreak is shown in Figure 11.1.

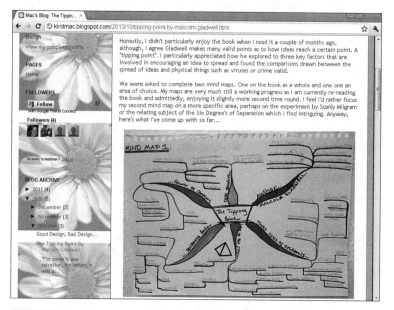

FIGURE 11.1   "Connectors" are people who start epidemics of thought and action.

Strong Facebook networkers don't just buy from you themselves; they encourage many others to do so as well, and everyone involved feels good about the process, reinforcing their relationship with you. One of these people can be worth her weight in gold—or at least worth spending a few hundred dollars a month to attract.

Give some thought to how much you might be willing to spend on a six-month trial of Facebook advertising; then throw yourself into it, or get some help to do so. Whether or not you decide that Facebook advertising and your business are a great match for you today, the experience and insights you gain will help you in assessing online opportunities for years to come.

Avoiding Wastage

In advertising, "wastage" is paying to advertise to customers who won't want what you're selling. For instance, television networks charge advertisers for delivering a certain number of viewers for their ads. If the ad is, say, female-oriented—women's shoes, perhaps—the male portion of the audience is wastage for that advertiser. Half of the "eyeballs" that the advertiser is paying for have no interest in the product. For a typical beer commercial, the opposite would be (mostly) true.

That's why a company selling women's shoes will concentrate its advertising around maybe a soap opera—so-named because the original advertisers were often soap companies who sold to housewives, the main people who were able to watch TV in the middle of the day. And a typical beer company will advertise heavily on sports, which has the right audience— men, and more than a few women, who are likely to be drinking beer while watching the ad itself.

For your advertising to be effective, you have to think about wastage a lot. Who are the people you really need to reach with your ad? How can you target them in ways that make sense for each medium? Television, radio, newspapers all have their own particular characteristics that work well for some target audiences and poorly for others.

Facebook is great for just about eliminating wastage. You can avoid paying to show your Ad to huge groups of people—men or women, younger or older, married or single. This is a huge win.

Also for most Facebook Ads, you don't even pay for showing them—you just pay when someone clicks the Ad. So you don't pay until someone in the right demographic group *and* who's interested takes notice. Not very much like the early TV ads with Cal Worthington and his dog Spot!

NOTE: **Demographic**

The word "demography" is Greek, and it combines *demos* (people) and *graphy* (a written representation; more recently, statistics). So "demographics" is "statistics about people."

Figure 11.2 shows a chart within an article about the "5M's of Advertising"—Mission, Money, Message, Media, and Measurement. Geographic targeting, for instance, is part of the Media bucket.

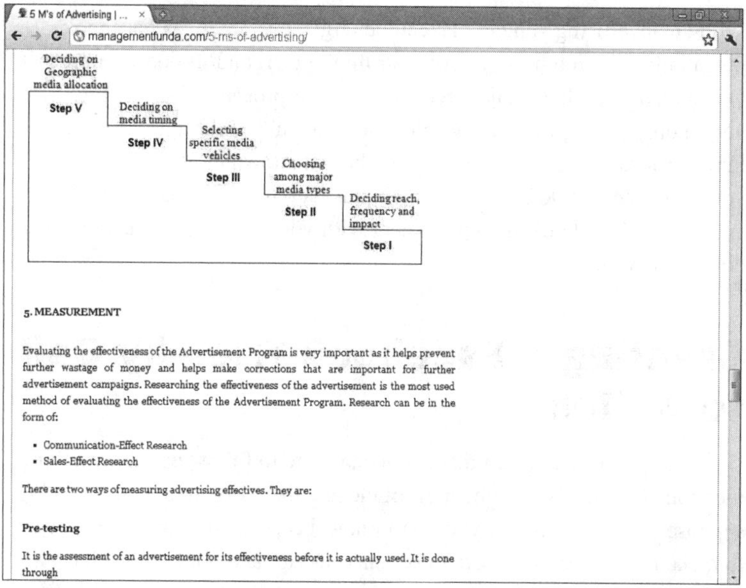

FIGURE 11.2   Getting your message out to just the right people is hard work.

The Facebook audience does have some limitations. The heaviest Facebook users are high school students, college students, and college-educated people young enough to have attended college in the Facebook era, which means roughly the last ten years. So that means the biggest chunk of the Facebook audience are relatively well-off 15- to 30-year-olds. And women outnumber men on the service—in the United States, by a ratio of about 55% to 45% at this writing.

But with 500 million users and growing, Facebook includes a lot of people beyond young, educated adults. You certainly can't use Facebook if you need to reach everyone who's coming up on retirement age. But you can use it to reach an awful lot of people who are—and with certainty that you're not spending your money on younger people. (Facebook requires you to enter the year of your birth when you sign up, although you don't have to display the year to other users. The result, though, is that Facebook knows your age.)

With an advertising vehicle that can be targeted as finely as Facebook potentially can, you have to turn your thinking around. It doesn't matter if you can only reach a small percentage of your prospects—as long as you're only paying to reach people who you really want to reach. You may, for instance, own an auto repair shop in a town of 30,000 people; if you only reach 1,000 of them, that sounds bad, but if it's the right 1,000, and 100 of them book an appointment with you next week, you've actually done very well.

Creating a Facebook-Friendly Call to Action

How many times have you made a mental note to follow up on something mentioned in an advertisement or article and then forgotten to act on it? (I suppose the answer is that you don't know, because you forgot.) You want to make it very easy for users to act on your Ad, and not let them have a chance to forget. This not only increases your Ad's effectiveness, but it also makes the effectiveness of the Ad much easier to track as well.

If the call to action in an Ad is "call now," you'll know right away if the Ad was effective. If the call to action is "stop by when you're in the neighborhood," you'll probably never know for sure if the Ad makes any difference.

A crucial observation for Facebook advertising is that Facebook users like to stay in Facebook. One anecdotal observation made by an advertiser was that people were four times more likely to go to a Facebook Page than to a comparable page on the Web. This kind of statistic will vary, depending on the group and the type of Ad, but in general, it's best to let people stay in Facebook as much as possible.

This is where all the other elements of your Facebook presence pay off. If you create an attractive Facebook fan page for your business, with a reasonable and growing number of Likes, and regular status updates from your personal page as well as your business page—that mention Facebook Deals as well as other news—then you can cheerfully link your Ad to your Facebook fan page. People will get a good impression of you throughout.

NOTE: Facebook Ads and Other Ads

If you do other advertising, how does Facebook fit into the mix? Two features stand out: Facebook ties into people's social networks very well, as described in this lesson and the next one; and Facebook Insights, Facebook's ad tracking tool, gives you excellent demographic information about your Facebook presence. (For more information, see Lesson 14, "Tracking the Performance of Your Facebook Presence.") So plan your Facebook Ads to "go viral" among people's friends and family and take advantage of Facebook Insights to track the results.

Designing an Ad

Facebook Ads are quite simple—you've noticed them and perhaps even clicked on one.

My own observation is that Facebook advertising is just about to take off. In a typical Facebook session, I don't usually see an attractive mix of relevant national, regional, and local Ads that makes the Ads as a whole interesting to me. I see mostly generic Ads that look like something from a mailed coupon circular.

The opportunity for you is to be one of the first of your group to break through the noise level with a carefully targeted Ad that intrigues people and draws clicks—then converts them into sales.

Facebook Ads are made up of four elements; three are visible and one is not:

▶ **Destination URL.** This is the location of the page users see when they click your Ad. On some browser setups, users see it if they mouse over the Ad. The Web page that people reach when they click is very important—you just paid money to get someone to visit it. The destination page has to help get the visitor to buy something, so you can start earning your money back!

▶ **Image.** For most new Facebook advertisers, the key to your Ad is the image you use. The size is quite small—about 100 pixels square—and can only have a few letters of text or one, simple, recognizable image (or both, if you're very clever). The image has to be eye-catching, but not shocking or weird, and has to relate strongly to the other elements of the Ad. A photo of the owner is one sensible approach.

▶ **Title.** This is only 25 letters (four or five words). It has to be intriguing and informative, but not come across as "hype." You can depend on the photo, to help orient people. "Special on Fresh Chicken" works well, especially if the image is the logo of a local grocery store. So does "2-for-1 Burger Tuesday," helped along by an image of a big, juicy burger.

▶ **Body text.** The body text is 125 characters, or about 25 words, of description. These words should give a detail or two that reassures the user that they want, and can get, the deal promised by the title. Aim for about 20 words here—more than that can look like too much. Here's an example, just 17 words long: "We have the best deal around on locally grown chicken. Today and tomorrow only; click for details."

Several Facebook Ads are shown in Figure 11.3. Note that the elements are called out.

Targeting Your Ads

Facebook allows reasonably fine targeting of your Ads—by location (down to the city level), by age, by gender, by gender interest, by type of relationship, by language, and by likes and interests. (Because it's free-form, the "likes and interests" part is the hardest to work with, but also the one with the most potential.)

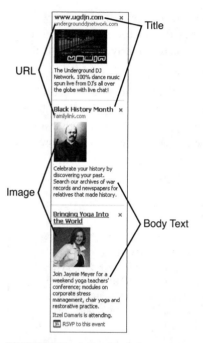

URL

Image

Title

Body Text

FIGURE 11.3   A Facebook Ad is simple, but getting it right is important.

NOTE: **Keyword Searches Work Well, Too**

While Facebook has many advantages, there are other ways to find potential customers using online marketing. One tool that's become very popular is search engine marketing, which is targeting search engine users by the search keywords they're using. You can actually combine Facebook Ads and search engine marketing for different kinds of promotional efforts. If you're interested in learning more about the leading search engine advertising tool, Google AdWords, see my book, *Sams Teach Yourself Google AdWords in 10 Minutes*.

You can choose to pay for your Ads by the number of people who view them, called PPV, or Pay Per View; or by the number of people who click them, which is called PPC, or Pay Per Click. You may want to try both methods and see which works better for you.

Try to avoid thinking of your Ads as reaching a share of the Facebook audience, or even a share of the audience you're looking for. Think instead of starting from zero; with an empty shopping basket, as it were. Every potential customer that you put in the basket—that is, who you show your Ad to—is someone with whom you want to engage. Think of these inter-actions as conversations, and see how far the conversation gets.

> TIP: **Start with a Rifle Shot**
>
> Advertising is usually described as a shotgun approach, implying that most of what you fire out there misses the target. If you have time and if you really want to stretch your Facebook advertising dol-lars, make your target audience very narrow at first—a rifle shot. If you're selling used cars, for instance, try targeting single males between 17 and 20, in your local area, a group that's very inter-ested in affordable cars and very close to you. Figure out what your conversion rate is for this group; then try to maintain a rate close to that as you broaden your Ad to reach a wider range of people.

Understanding How Facebook Determines a User's Location

There's an old saying that there are three important things in running a business: location, location, and location. The most important thing for Facebook Ads is location as well.

In most countries, you can target your Facebook Ads down to the city level. You can also set a radius around a city to include nearby suburbs and smaller cities and towns. This allows you to only pay for people who are in the geographical target area for your Ad.

It's worth knowing a bit about how Facebook does this, given you'll be paying for it. Every computer that uses the Internet has a numeric code called an IP address. This IP address has a physical location attached to it, which is usually but not always correct—so you won't get 100% compliance on your location-targeted Ads.

If a Facebook user has a home address listed in his profile—many do, even though some of us don't recommend it—Facebook will use that instead. If the user is at a different location than his home address when your Ad is up for display, you might prefer that Facebook use the person's current location, his listed home location, or even both. You don't have the option, though; you get the user's home location—if he has entered one—or his current location, if not.

This is a small enough problem for you not to worry about it much. The great majority of the people you reach with location-based targeting will either be currently in your target area or be from there in the fairly recent past. Just check the effectiveness of your Ad, as described in Lesson 13, "Promoting Your Facebook Presence," and don't spend too much money on packages that aren't working.

Focusing on Major Types of Targeting

Following is a brief description of the major targeting types that Facebook allows. Facebook is very good indeed at the first types of targeting: location, age, birthday, gender, relationship status, and languages. These are major identifiers for people, and Facebook has reliable information on them.

Facebook also offers targeting by likes and interests, but the information Facebook has here tends to be sketchy. It's assembled one Like at a time, so it isn't comprehensive. It may be worth experimenting with, but is not as reliable as the more detailed biographical information.

As you enter your targeting criteria, Facebook displays the estimated number of people (adults over 18) who could conceivably see your Ad (if you give Facebook enough money, that is). For the United States, before using any targeting, that number will be well over 125 million people. Watch the number drop as you enter targeting criteria so that you're sure someone will get to see your Ad!

Think of how you might assemble the relevant categories into a package that precisely targets your audience. The major types of targeting are:

▶ **Location.** You can specify a country; a state or province; and, in some countries, a city. (City targeting is only available in the United States, Canada, and the UK at this writing.) When you pick a city, you can also specify a radius around the city to include nearby small cities and suburbs. Target as narrowly as you can at first, and then expand your range after your Ad shows that it's paying for itself.

▶ **Age and birthday.** Facebook begins by targeting all users over 18, but you can fine-tune this down to one year at a time if you want to. This is a huge opportunity to creatively target offers to specific groups. Divide the whole age range into, say, 5-year chunks and figure out which ones are in your overall target audience and which are most likely to respond to a specific combination of an offer and creative to convey it. ("Creative" is the ad industry term for the ad itself—what people see and, for radio and TV ads, hear.) In particular, take advantage of Facebook's strength with young people to reach potential customers under 30. You can also create special birthday offers that only appear to people on their birthdays.

▶ **Gender and relationships.** You can target Ads by gender, by whether a person is interested in men or women, and by whether a person is single, in a relationship, engaged, or married. These choices are listed under "Advanced Targeting Options," but you should always consider them. While avoiding overly "cute" or stereotypical approaches, you can target your Ads appropriately for your audience. Combining gender and relationship status with age really lets you narrow your focus.

▶ **Education level.** You can target Ads to all education levels or to college grads (about 25% of Facebook's total in the United States at this writing), current college students (a bit less than 10%), or current high school students (about 2%). For the right products and services, this can be very useful targeting, allowing you to make comparisons, test market to specific groups, and so on.

All types of targeting listed here have two things in common:

▶ They represent major advertising categories that have been used for decades and are well-studied and well-understood groups.

▶ Facebook has highly reliable information on them.

Facebook offers other kinds of targeting that are less "solid" but potentially useful in specific circumstances.

> TIP: **Using the Ad Creator for Testing**
>
> Use the Ad creation page, described in the next lesson, for testing out ideas. When you specify the URL, title, body text and image, Facebook creates a sample Ad. When you enter demographic targeting criteria, Facebook shows you the number of people you'll reach using those criteria. Get the Ad example and the estimated reach from the page, print them out, and discuss before committing to an Ad and accompanying targeting.

Minor Types of Targeting

Facebook also offers targeting using newer, "emerging" categories. These categories are based on two different types of entries the user makes, both somewhat fuzzy:

▶ Words entered by the user or observed by Facebook. The Likes & Interests category described here falls into this category. It gives you the opportunity to enter words and phrases, describing likes and interests, that the user may have entered about herself— or potentially that emerge from her online behavior. Unfortunately, neither is anywhere close to exact; for example, are "psychologist," "therapist," or "counselor" the same thing, or different? Not to mention misspellings that people might make. The same applies to workplaces to a lesser extent. For example, "IBM" might seem simple enough, but some people spell it out, and the company has many brands, divisions, and so on.

▶ Connections to specific pages, events, groups, and apps you manage and to workplaces. This is a tool for reaching people who are already connected to your Facebook Pages, or for showing them a different Ad than shown to the masses.

Here are the categories you see when setting up a Facebook Ad that are not major demographic categories, but looser or very small groups instead:

▶ **Likes and interests.** Facebook offers targeting by likes and interests, but the information Facebook is likely to have is pretty incomplete, in my opinion. Many Facebook users don't enter such information and don't do enough with their whole range of interests in Facebook (at least not yet) for Facebook to be able to infer it reliably. I recommend getting really good with the better-characterized standard categories listed here before trying to target by likes, interests, and so on.

▶ **Connections.** Facebook lets you target users who are or aren't connected to specific pages, events, and so on that you manage. Use this to help your Ad find—or avoid finding—people who are already connected to you.

▶ **Languages.** You can target by language, but unfortunately, not everyone provides this information. (About two million people among U.S. Facebook users list Spanish as a language spoken, but the actual number must be far higher.) However, it might be valuable for some very targeted approaches or trial runs.

TIP: **Vary Your Ad by Demographic Group**

Even if you're selling the same product or type of product to everyone, you can use different ad text and images for different demographic groups. For instance, you can have different Ads for younger people, older people, single people, or couples. You can craft both your offer and the look of each Ad to appeal to a specific target audience.

Summary

As a method for planning your advertisements, you learned in this lesson how to budget for your Facebook Ads, how to target your Ads to avoid "wastage," and how to design your Ads. In the next lesson, you learn how to price your Ads and how to create your ad campaign.

LESSON 12
Pricing and Creating Your Ad Campaign

In this lesson, you learn about Facebook Ad costs, key terms for online advertising, and how to create your Ad on Facebook.

Understanding What You Pay

The framework for how online advertising works has largely been set by Google. Google's AdWords service allows advertisers to bid on general search terms, such as "ice cream," and narrow ones, such as "ice cream San Francisco." It also allows you to bid on the term "ice cream" within a specific geographic area, such as certain ZIP codes in San Francisco.

Facebook's approach is quite similar to Google's, but Google's is more mature and generates nearly all of Google's tens of billions of dollars in annual profit. Facebook, which started much later, is not nearly as successful...yet. But Facebook's Ad business is growing fast.

You need to know this Google/Facebook comparison for two reasons. The first is that Facebook's help information and support for Facebook advertising, as well as a lot of third-party information such as books, assumes that you're familiar with Google's approach before you start using Facebook's Ads. So the assumption is that you'll easily understand Facebook's approach, which is less complex than Google's offering.

If you're a true newbie to online advertising and are using Facebook as your first effort, you're a bit out of luck—except for here in this book. As the author of *Sams Teach Yourself Google AdWords in 10 Minutes*, I'm well-versed in AdWords, and I understand that both Google AdWords and Facebook Ads are quite challenging at first. The learning curve is steep and expensive; you literally pay, in real money, for any mistakes you make along the way.

So I explain carefully here how to get started with Facebook advertising by defining the key terms and describing how to guard yourself against problems. With this knowledge in hand, you'll not only be ready to do well with Facebook Ads, but you'll know much of what you need to know to use Google AdWords effectively as well if you decide to add it to your toolbox. Most businesses should probably use both.

> CAUTION: **Check Your Facebook Ads Spending**
>
> Check your Facebook Ads spending carefully and confirm that it's still meeting your goals on a daily basis. Otherwise, it's all too easy to let a month or two go by and get hit with a bill for hundreds or thousands of dollars for a campaign that is not paying off for your business.

With all this learning to do and potential expense, why bother? It's because every new generation of advertising creates winners and losers. Mail-order catalogs, the Yellow Pages, radio, television, Internet selling, and Google AdWords have all helped make or break businesses. Think of how the independent bookstore sector has shrunk in the face of the success of Amazon.com and the Kindle. It's very easy for you to win big with Facebook advertising—or to lose big, if competitors figure it out before you do.

This book is unusual in giving you a chance to get on top of Facebook advertising and start using it to your advantage while it's still early. If you have at least a modest program in place in the near future, you're likely to be well ahead of your competition—and safe from surprises.

Learning Key Advertising Terms

The most famous saying about advertising is attributed to early U.S. department store king John Wanamaker, and it goes like this: "Half the money I spend on advertising is wasted; the trouble is, I don't know which half." Tracking the results of advertising has always been a problem; who knows exactly how many sales a billboard, for instance, generates? But online advertising has the potential to largely solve this conundrum.

There are seven key online advertising terms you need to understand to spend your online advertising money wisely:

- ▶ **Creative.** This is not a religious term; "the creative" simply refers to the part of the ad that the potential customer actually sees and/or hears. For a TV ad, the creative is what you see and hear for perhaps 30 or 60 seconds. For a Facebook Ad, the creative includes not only an image, a title, and body text; it also includes any specialized Facebook pages or Web pages you create to show to people who click the Ad.

- ▶ **Demographic** or **demographics.** This is the subset of all Facebook users (or of the general population) that you want to get your Ad in front of. "We want to hit the college female and elderly demographics with this campaign." It's wonderful for a long-time advertiser to be able to get rid of huge swathes of people from their target audience—and from their ad budgeting—just by clicking a few buttons, as one can do in Facebook Ads, Google AdWords, and other online advertising vehicles.

- ▶ **Cost per click (CPC).** This term is key to the success of most online advertising. As the advertiser, you only pay for an ad when someone clicks it. Although there's no set figure or range, it can be useful to think of CPCs as being around $1 per click for many campaigns. At a CPC of $1, if 100 people click your ad, and no one buys, you just wasted $100.

The ad service provider—Google, Facebook, and so on—will show your ad many times and never charge you except when someone clicks. When someone does click, it's relatively easy to track the results, and to know if your advertising is making or losing money for you.

It's not a perpetual free ride; if no one ever clicks your ad, your provider is not making any money from you, and they'll drop your ad. But initially the risk is on them, not you, if your ad doesn't attract clicks.

▶ **Cost per thousand (CPM).** Cost per thousand impressions, or viewings, is a term from broadcast, newspaper, and magazine advertising. CPM refers to ads that are paid for by the number of times they're shown, not the number of times they're clicked. (M is the Roman numeral for "one thousand.") We won't talk much about CPM advertising here, because CPC advertising is much more frequently used and is considered to be more effective for online advertising than using CPM-based approaches.

▶ **Click-through ratio (CTR).** This is the percentage of showings of your ad that result in clicks. Again, there's no set ratio, but think of a CTR of 1% or 2% as being a kind of target for many campaigns. (I'd be surprised if many of the Facebook Ads I've seen are reaching this kind of CTR figure yet.)

▶ **Maximum bid.** When you say how much you'll pay for a click (or for a thousand viewings), you don't just set a price you'll pay; you specify a maximum bid. You usually get charged an average cost that's somewhat less than your maximum.

▶ **Daily budget.** This is simply the maximum figure you agree to spend per day as people click your ad. Your ad probably won't show every time it normally could because the daily budget stops it from running as often as it otherwise would. Facebook also allows you to set a lifetime budget—your ad runs continuously throughout each day, as many times as possible, until the lifetime budget is spent.

So here's a summary of how you budget for an online advertising campaign with these terms noted: You do the *creative* for one or more ads. The ad, or ads, are intended to reach key *demographics* who are considered likely to buy your product.

Using the Facebook advertising set-up page, you enter the creative and figure out the *CPC* (or, in some cases, *CPM*) you'll pay to get your Ad shown. You specify a *maximum bid* (Facebook will recommend this to you) and set your *daily budget* to limit your spending. Facebook then tracks the number of times it shows the Ad and the number of clicks, and reports these back, along with the CTR that the Ad achieved.

NOTE: **(M)ad Talk**

Why is there a hit series about advertising called *Mad Men*? Because the home of several top advertising agencies during the advertising boom of the 1960s, fueled by the rise of color television, was New York's Madison Avenue and the surrounding area. Madison Avenue was the Silicon Valley of its day, full of bright, creative people making lots of money and getting lots of public attention. Several of the terms that we're using here were coined, or at least put into widespread use, back then.

You then review your sales results and costs and adjust any and all of this to get the results you want.

Creating an Ad

Here's a brief guide for actually creating a Facebook Ad. Review the steps carefully before you begin and refer to previous sections in this lesson so you can be ready to see the process through to completion:

1. From your Home page (which shows your News Feed), click the link on the left-hand side: **Ads and Pages**. If that link is not visible to you, click the **Advertising** link at the bottom of the page.

   A list of pages you administer appears.

2. Click the green **Create an Ad** button.

   The Design Your Ad page appears.

3. Enter the destination URL. If the URL is for your Facebook fan page, you will need to choose Facebook Ads (the more likely choice) or Sponsored Stories; then choose the Destination Tab for the user to arrive at on your fan page.

   This is the URL the user goes to when he clicks the Ad. It should be a page that takes the user straight into whatever you want him to do—call you, Like something on Facebook, buy something, and so on. It should also have a "look and feel" similar to the Ad so the user feels a sense of continuity.

4. If you wish, click the **Suggest an Ad** button.

A suggested ad appears, as shown in Figure 12.1. Facebook will go to the web page specified by the destination URL and assemble information to suggest an ad for you. It allows you to choose from the images on the destination page and gets text from the top of the page. It's not likely to be perfect, but should give you some ideas.

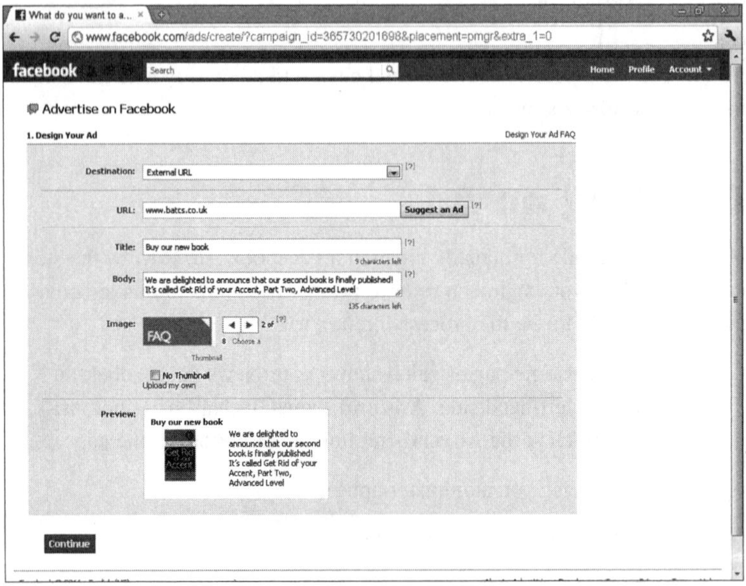

FIGURE 12.1   Facebook will suggest an ad for you.

5. Enter the Ad title (25 characters or fewer).

This should tell the user, in four or five words of unemotional language, what she's going to get out of reading (and perhaps clicking) the Ad. A Facebook Ad from the USC Masters of Teaching program has the title: "Want to be a teacher?" This is perfect.

TIP: **Optimizing Your Ad**

To make your Ad great, consider experimenting with different titles, body text, and images until you find the combination that works best. Comparing one version directly to another for effectiveness is called *A/B testing* or *split testing*.

6. Enter the body text (135 characters or fewer).

    This is supporting information that spells out the promise made by the title. For instance, when I see that a teacher's training program is at USC—500 miles away from me—I automatically discount it unless the program is described as "online." Give specific dates and times if they matter. And try not to use all 135 characters (about 25 words)—try to keep it less than 20 words, which should keep you within 5 lines of text in the display Ad. To me, at least, six lines of text just looks like too much.

7. Choose an image file. Click **Continue**.

    The image file should be up to 110 x 80 pixels, but it may be cropped to as small as 100 x 72 pixels, so don't put vital information or parts of a graphic on the edges. The image should be clearly visible from a distance and tied to your product or service, your body text, and the destination the user reaches if he clicks your Ad. Don't shrink an image with text that is thereby made unreadable—it's frustrating and looks lazy.

    As you enter the title, text, and image, a preview of the Ad appears. Keep working on the text and image until you have an Ad that's attractive and professional. Ask others for their opinions and for proofreading help.

8. Begin entering targeting options, as shown in Figure 12.2. Specifying the country and, if available and needed, whether to target the whole country; states, provinces, and regions; or a city. For a city, specify whether to also include other cities within 10, 20, or 50 miles.

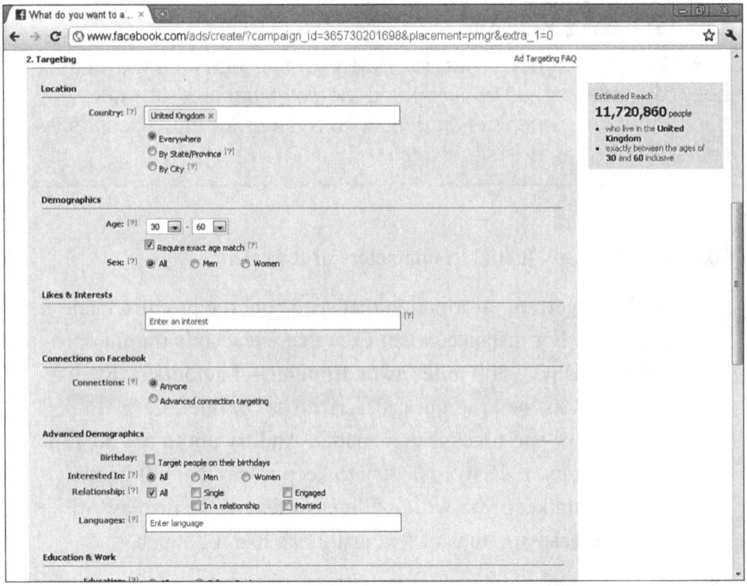

FIGURE 12.2   Target by location, simple demographics, and potentially by likes and interests.

As you specify the location your Ad will run in, the estimated reach will update to reflect the choices you make.

9. Specify the age range for your Ad. Click the checkbox for **Require Exact Age Match** if you're serious about your range. If you want to let Facebook be somewhat fuzzy and show discounted Ads that are a bit outside your range, at a discount, don't check the box.

CAUTION: **Be Careful with Kids**

Be very careful before advertising to (the word "targeting" sounds bad here) people under 18, which includes most high school students. Consider taking advice from lawyers and marketers with relevant experience before proceeding, as the legal complexities, and people's sensitivities, are far higher for high schoolers than for adults. Facebook does not allow people under 13 to become users.

---

10. Specify whether the Ad should go to All people, Men only, or Women only.

    This is very useful for targeting just men or just women for a given product—or for using different Ads for the same product. However, a few Facebook users—about 1%, in the U.S.—don't state whether they're men or women, and Facebook doesn't include a "decline to state" category. So the only way to reach absolutely everyone is to choose "all."

11. If you choose to, enter **Likes & Interests** information.

    If you want to target people who like certain music groups, for instance, start entering names here. Not every user enters this kind of information, though, so your reach will drop sharply if you use this kind of targeting.

12. If you choose, target **Connections**.

    You can use this area to target users who are or aren't already connected to a page that you're the administrator for. This way you can try to get new members for a group, for instance, without haranguing existing members. Or you can do different Ads for people who are or aren't already a member of the group.

13. If you choose to do so, click the **Show Advanced Targeting Options** link. This will allow you to specify Advanced Demographics: Birthday-only targeting; relationship interest in All, Men, or Women; type of relationship; and Languages.

    The options are shown in Figure 12.2. Remember that you can use these fields to target different ad creative to different people within your overall target audience.

14. If you click the **Show Advanced Targeting Options** link, you can also target by Education & Work. You can target by education—All, College Grad, In College, or In High School—or by specific workplaces. Click **Continue**.

    These options are shown in Figure 12.3.

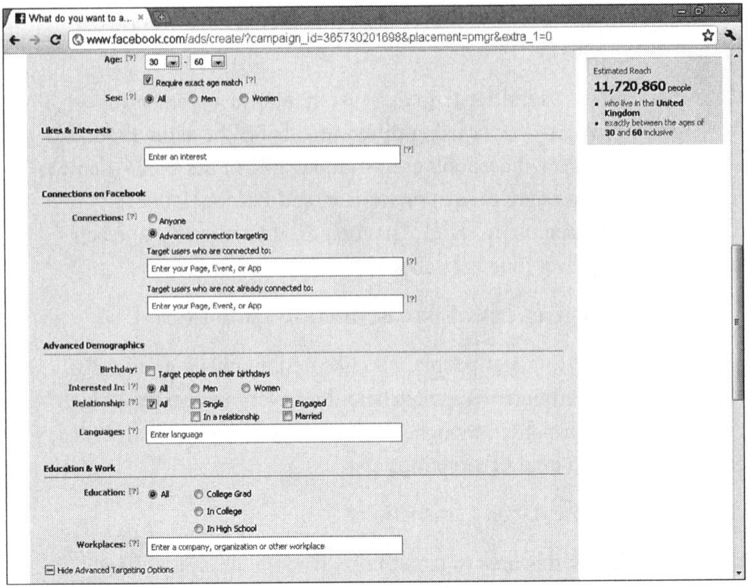

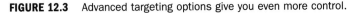

FIGURE 12.3   Advanced targeting options give you even more control.

15. Enter pricing and scheduling options. Start with the pull-down for **Account Currency**, **Country/Territory** (for billing, not for Ad targeting), and **Time Zone**.

These options are shown in Figure 12.4.

16. Enter a Campaign Name.

An example of a campaign name is 2005 Cabernet/Men. This would be for advertising a vintage wine, with different versions of the creative for men and women. (If selling alcohol, be sure you target people above the legal drinking age in your targeting options!)

17. Enter a Budget, the amount you're willing to spend Per day or a Total for the whole campaign.

I have personal experience that this type of thing is a very easy way to spend money. So be very careful about setting this up.

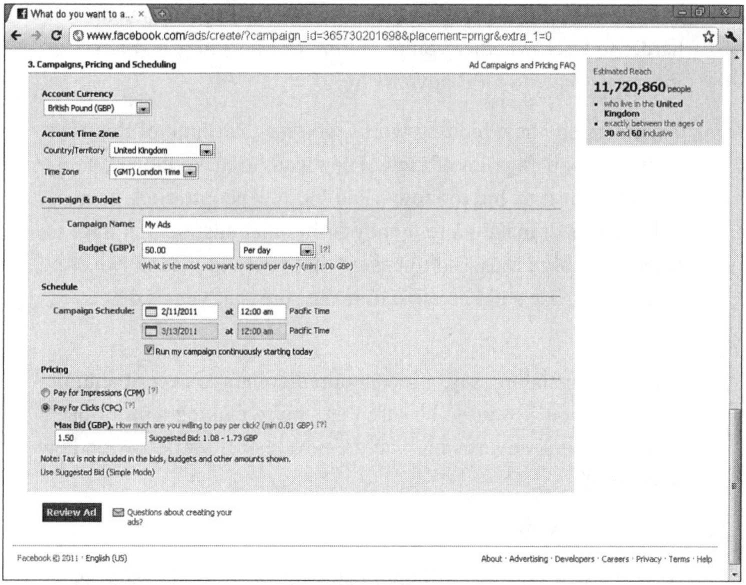

FIGURE 12.4 Ka-ching—specify where your money is going.

What you really need is a daily limit and a total limit, but that's not offered. So monitor your spending, and the results you're getting for the money, very carefully.

18. Enter the Campaign Schedule, the start and stop days and times for the campaign. Click to set the checkbox for **Run My Campaign Continuously Starting Today**.

19. Review the Pricing, the suggested bid per click that Facebook sets.

Facebook sets you up for paying for every click of your Ad and sets the suggested amount for you.

20. If you choose to do so, click the **Set a Different Bid (Advanced Mode)** link. You can specify Pay for Impressions (CPM), which is TV-type advertising, or Pay for Clicks (CPC), which is more Internet-style advertising. You can also specify your Max Bid.

I suggest leaving CPM advertising to the experts. It's much harder to track whether you're getting results with CPM advertising than it is with CPC advertising.

To understand how bidding works, you have to think of things from Facebook's point of view. They want to make money, so if you set your max bid too low—and too few people click your Ad—they will make more money from other ads. So you have to set a fairly high Max Bid to ensure that your Ad gets shown. And you have to use solid creative to make sure that your Ad gets clicked.

It's worth spending, say, a few hundred dollars to experiment, but after that, you'll want to be sure that you're making a profit on your Facebook advertising. See the next lesson for details on how to do that.

21. Click **Review Ad**.

A preview of your Ad and your campaign settings appears, as shown in Figure 12.5.

FIGURE 12.5   Your Ad is ready to roll.

> CAUTION: **A Good Time to Read the Fine Print**
>
> Carefully review the small warning text at the bottom of the screen. It reminds you that you can have your Ads cancelled and your Facebook account terminated if you break Facebook's rules. It can be tempting to push the boundaries in advertising to get attention, and it can be easy to forget that what's considered funny among one group of people might be considered offensive by another. Be careful, especially when you're starting out, and get help in reviewing the Ad if you feel it's needed.

22. Click **Edit Ad** to do more work on the Ad or **Place Order** to start the Ad. You will then be asked to enter your credit card or PayPal information.

Your Ad is likely to start running soon after you submit it. However, you may not see it even if you're in the target demographic; your budget may not be sufficient to get the Ad shown to every qualified Facebook user who comes along—including yourself!

Summary

In this lesson, you learned how to create your Facebook Ads, including the integral considerations of what you pay for your Facebook Ads and what the key terms are for online advertising. In the next lesson, you learn how to promote your entire Facebook presence.

LESSON 13

Promoting Your Facebook Presence

In this lesson, you learn why promotion is important. You also see how to measure the impact of your efforts and how to promote your Facebook presence in the real world as well as online.

Understanding Why Promotion Is Important

Promoting your Facebook presence is important. Why?

It used to be common for people to hang out at the general store, the post office, the barber shop, or the hair salon to chat and exchange news. These businesses were a part of their customers' lives. In some places, when the local grocery store or post office closes, people say, "Well, there goes our community."

But people have found community in other ways—largely online, and largely on Facebook. Many younger people check their Facebook Pages dozens of times a day. Even their elders often feel they can't go too long without checking in.

Your purpose in putting your business on Facebook is to share in this enormous energy, to create an online community of your own around your business. (Maybe even a big one, depending on how ambitious you are!) People who are involved in this community are more likely to buy from you and to promote you to their networks of friends, family members, and coworkers. People who are, instead, in the community of a competitor are less likely to buy from you.

Promoting your Facebook presence is important to growing your community, making it more fun and more interesting. In high tech, this is called the "network effect"—an online property becomes more valuable to each of its users, the more users it has.

There's also a cost/benefit side to the equation. It's a fair amount of work to create, maintain, and improve your Facebook presence. You have to do much of the work whether you have a few dozen people visiting you or a thousand. A small amount of additional promotional effort can help build the number of people visiting you, giving you a lot more payback for your efforts.

Finally, Facebook is hot. People who use it consistently are very invested in thinking it's important—because if it's not, they're wasting their time. They want and need to hear that you're on Facebook and see you there to help their world make sense. Otherwise, if they can meet their needs in a way that's more in tune with their Facebook exertions, they will.

Even people who don't use Facebook much know it's hot—they hear about it from friends and family and see it in books, magazines, even as the focus (sorry for the pun) of an Oscar-winning movie. So when you promote your Facebook presence, they're impressed—you've made it clear that you're on top of what's happening, for your business and in the world at large. This increases their trust in doing business with you. And if and when they do get on Facebook, they're likely to seek you out.

So the reasons for promoting your business's Facebook presence can be summed up as

▶ Growing your Facebook community (and with it, your business).

▶ Leveraging your Facebook investment across more visitors.

▶ Creating a positive impression of your business with all your customers.

The online site Mashable.com sums it up well: "Do whatever it takes to let people know that you're on Facebook and you want them to become a part of your community."

Measuring Your Efforts

There's a famous saying in management: "That which gets measured gets done." The next and final lesson in this book tells you specifics about how to measure the impact of your Facebook presence, but here are some big-picture measures you will want to keep an eye on as well:

▶ **Likes.** How many people Like you on Facebook? People measure their social success by their Facebook friends; businesses measure their promotional success by their Facebook Likes. Work hard to keep growing your number of Likes. Blisstree, a magazine-style site for women, puts **Become a Fan** buttons on every page. They're running a contest giving a pair of designer sandals to a "Like"r, and they wrote a whole article just to appeal for Facebook Likes and followers on Twitter, as shown in Figure 13.1.

FIGURE 13.1   Blisstree really wants you to like them on Facebook.

▶ **Comments.** You know that people are engaged with you when they comment on your status updates or respond to your comments on other people's comments. So track how many comments you get.

▶ **Response to offers.** Make offers on Facebook and see how many people respond. You can be quite casual about this—"mention that you saw us on Facebook today to get a free bonus" is enough. You know you're truly succeeding when people who aren't on Facebook hear the news, and claim they are, to get in on the bonus.

▶ **Mentions.** Mentions of your Facebook presence in the real world will probably be rare, but they're invaluable. Ask people who work for your business or who you know to alert you to any mentions they hear about your Facebook presence—good or bad. It's not quite true that "there's no such thing as bad publicity," but close enough.

Promoting in the Real World

Ideally, you want every contact that people have with your business to include a reminder that you're on Facebook—or a specific invitation to see you there.

Here are some ways to promote your Facebook presence in the real world:

▶ **Put your Facebook presence on your business card.** Add a line similar to the following to your business card: "Facebook: www. facebook.com/MyBusiness." This will impress everyone and alert Facebook users that they won't be wasting their time if they look for you on Facebook.

▶ **Get Facebook-themed business cards.** You can get business cards made up that have a Facebook theme. One company that offers them is Zazzle, as you can see in Figure 13.2.

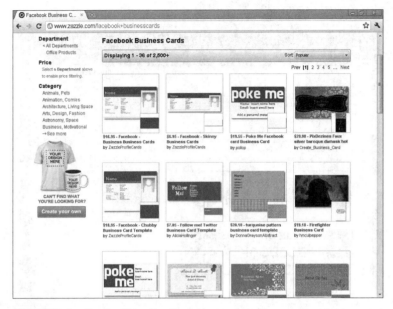

FIGURE 13.2 Zazzle offers Facebook business cards.

▶ **Create a Facebook-specific business card.** You can have a business card made up that promotes your Facebook presence only. A sporting goods company called Tubes has done this, shown in Figure 13.3.

TIP: **QR Codes**

If you see an odd-looking, squiggly square like the one in the lower-right corner of the business card in Figure 13.3, it's probably a Quick Reference code, called a QR code for short. QR codes can put text information, such as a potentially long URL, into a small space. A program such as an app on your smartphone can then decode the QR code and take you to the website.

▶ **Put your Facebook presence on stationery and in Ads.** At least add your Facebook Page address as it is on your business cards. If you have space, add a few encouraging words, such as "Visit us on Facebook!"

FIGURE 13.3   BrimBase writes about the virtues of having a business card just for Facebook.

▶ **Run explicit Facebook promotions.** Conduct a contest or raffle via Facebook and advertise it. For instance, "Like us on Facebook to win free ice cream once a week all summer!" is a pretty tempting offer. You might get dozens of Likes for a cost of $40 or $50.

▶ **Promote checking in.** When people are in your shop or other business, promote checking in. Enter people into a contest or raffle or just ask people if they've checked in. You can even call out when you're crowded, "Who's checked in?" and offer a free cookie or other goodie to people who are. Or make an offer: "Come in, check in, and win!"

Keep your efforts going. I was once involved in testing some advertising with a focus group. The intention of the focus group members to purchase our product didn't start to increase until we'd shown them the same ad three times! This seems illogical—the ad hadn't changed. But people hear so many advertising and promotional messages today that repetition is crucial to getting your message across. Yes, saying things over and over is really, really important.

Promoting Online and on Facebook

When people are online, they're only a click away from your Facebook presence. When people aren't already in Facebook, though—when they're reading email, or on your website—they might be a little reluctant to go there. Facebook has gained a reputation as the world's greatest time sink, and people sometimes avoid going there too often for just that reason.

So you've got two jobs in promoting your Facebook presence in online venues that aren't within Facebook itself:

▶ **Letting people know that you're on Facebook.** Just letting people know that you're on Facebook is a plus point all by itself. They may then visit spontaneously at some later time.

▶ **Giving them a reason to come see your Facebook Page.** You'll get more visits if you motivate people to visit your Facebook Page.

To let people know you're on Facebook, include a tag line at the bottom of your email messages: "Come **see us** on Facebook!" or something similar. Turn the words "see us" into a link to your Facebook Page.

To encourage them to visit right away, though, use a bit of promotion. Something like this: "We're on Facebook! **Like** us to win!" This text is a bit cheesier, but it suggests to people that they can participate just by clicking a few times—once on the link, once on the Like button, and then the Back button on their browsers.

While you only want to put one line in your email signature, you can put more information on your website, as with the example of a blog post mentioning Twitter and Facebook, shown previously in Figure 13.1.

Getting people who aren't already on Facebook to come visit you there is great. It's easier, though, to get people who are already on Facebook to visit.

Here are the main ways to get people to spend some of their Facebook time with you:

▶ **Run ads.** Facebook Ads, described in the previous lesson, are great for driving intra-Facebook traffic to your page. A compelling offer, such as a lottery entry for Liking your page, will help get people to click. (The title text could be, "Like Us and Win!")

▶ **Write status updates.** Your status updates are an invitation to people who already Like your page to interact with you, so keep your updates current. If you write a particularly interesting, clever, or compelling update—such as a discount for mentioning a code, today only—people will share it as well, attracting more Likes.

The status updates for the popular online game Farmville are very focused—every post asks people to Like their Facebook Page. A typical page of Farmville status updates is shown in Figure 13.4.

▶ **Keep your personal profile updated.** Don't make your personal profile a marketing page for your business, but your personal updates—even the strictly personal ones—will bring your business to your friend's minds as well. Keeping your personal profile updated also shows you "walking the talk," being sincere with your overall commitment to Facebook.

▶ **Liking breeds liking.** When I visit a friend's Facebook Wall or a page they recommended to me, I see their Likes in a rotating line-up in the upper-right area of the page. So if I like (small "l") someone well enough to visit her page, I'm likely (no pun intended) to be favorably impressed by something they Like—and to Like it, too. This is the kind of chain reaction that Facebook is great for.

FIGURE 13.4   A Farmville codes page never stops mentioning Liking their page.

Use these techniques separately and in combination. Some of your Facebook Ads should lead directly to sales; others can be targeted toward building your online community. Status updates (for your personal page and for the business's page) can be fun, friendly, or businesslike. Stay within Facebook's informal and relaxed tone, but keep an eye on what your activity is doing for your business.

CAUTION: **Avoid Spamming**

One of the touchiest issues in online promotions is spam, which is short for "self-propelled advertising material." Any advertising that you send out, such as an email promotion, that's regarded as unwanted and intrusive will be regarded by at least some of the recipients as spam. Even a cheesy-looking Facebook Ad can seem "spammy." So keep it clean, keep it classy, and only advertise or email where you believe your message will be welcome.

Promoting All Your Facebook Pieces

You should promote and cross-promote all the parts of your Facebook presence. Of course, the more you do on Facebook, the more tools you have to work with. Use everything you do to promote everything else you do:

- ▶ **Interact around apps (see Lesson 3).** People like to interact around their Facebook apps. Get appropriate apps for both your personal profile and your business page.

- ▶ **Publish plenty of status updates (see Lesson 2).** After people Like you, they see your status updates. This applies to Facebook friends for your personal Facebook profile as well as people who Like the Facebook Page for your business. However, if there isn't much interaction, your status updates drop off the friends/Likers page. So be interesting—even entertaining—and interact with your fans and friends.

- ▶ **Get Likes (see Lesson 5).** Getting Likes for your page is the key to promoting your Facebook presence and to getting results from Facebook. As the quote from Mashable at the beginning of this lesson says, do everything you can to get Likes.

- ▶ **Get check-ins to your Places page (see Lesson 9).** Promote check-ins. I like keeping the Places page and the Facebook Page separate so there are two targets for different types of promotions. Some people will be comfortable with one but not the other; cater to both groups. You can add "check in and win" type messages to various marketing pieces, stationery, and so on.

- ▶ **Make a big deal of Deals (see Lesson 10).** Your Facebook Deals shouldn't end with the Deal itself. Only a small percentage of your customers and online friends will ever take advantage of a Deal directly, but all of them should hear about it. Publicize your Deals on Facebook; consider putting up a sign with Deal results in your business.

▶ **Promote your Ads (see Lesson 11).** You can promote your Ads. Put a code in your Ad and give people a discount for telling it back to you. Let people know when you've advertised—they like seeing a company they support getting the word out.

Summary

In this lesson, you learned why promotion is important, how to measure the impact of your efforts, and how to promote your Facebook presence in the real world and online. In the next lesson, you learn how to track statistics about users' interaction with your Facebook presence.

Tracking the Performance of Your Facebook Presence

In this lesson, you learn why tracking your Facebook presence is important. This includes how Facebook can provide you with accurate demographic information, how to use the Page Overview in Insights, and how to use the detail pages for Users and Interactions.

Understanding Why Tracking Is Important

In the previous lesson, I referred to the famous quote by John Wanamaker about knowing that half his advertising money was being wasted. (He just didn't know which half.) Tracking is the answer to that infamous conundrum of advertising. Within Facebook, you actually have the opportunity to know, with good precision, whether your advertising is paying off—and to quickly stop running the ads and placements that aren't.

Armed with this knowledge, you can ensure that your advertising is always profitable. You can set a target and say that you'll only spend a dollar on advertising if it brings you back two dollars in profit—and make it stick. Getting beyond guesswork is a big step in marketing.

The trouble is, as a business owner, you have lots of other things to do besides create and track advertising. So you have to do it efficiently, or you won't be able to do it at all. That's what Facebook's tracking tools (and this book) are all about—making it easy and efficient for you to know what advertisements and other elements of your Facebook presence are working for you.

Facebook Insights is the core tool for tracking your results on Facebook. This kind of software is known as analytics software because it helps you analyze your results. For comparison, Google has a similar (but more comprehensive) tool called, somewhat predictably, Google Analytics.

Getting analytics software for free—and having the data entered for you automatically, as part of a service—is revolutionary in marketing. People have paid many thousands of dollars for quite simple analyses in the past. You can do much better, for free, with Facebook Insights.

This lesson concentrates on helping you understand and use Facebook Insights. However, you should identify metrics and related information that are important to you, but not tracked by Facebook Insights, and track those as well. For instance, you may want to keep a record of comments made by people about your advertising, or tie Facebook analytics to actual sales. For any of this, you'll need to figure out what you want to record and then track those additional results outside of Facebook Insights.

Understanding Why Facebook Data Is So Accurate

The demographic data you get on Facebook is the best you're likely to get in any marketing you do—far better than on any other online source. That makes Facebook's Insights statistics capability a very powerful tool.

Here's what's different about Facebook, for marketing information purposes:

- ▶ **Users are logged in as themselves.** This is huge. Facebook is rare in being a very large online site that you can't usefully visit without being logged in.

- ▶ **Facebook users enter demographic data.** Facebook asks users to enter a small amount of highly personal demographic data. And because people interact with friends and family in Facebook, they're very highly motivated to be honest.

▶ **Facebook tracks pageviews precisely.** Facebook Pages are fairly simple—not a lot of Web 2.0 wizardry going on, as with the Instant Search on Google that's constantly changing the results as you type. So pageviews are easy to count and to map to specific users and their demographic data.

All this may seem simple enough, but the result is a real treasure trove of highly accurate information—accurate within a couple of percentage points, anyway, which in marketing is high precision indeed.

For comparison, Google AdWords gives you a lot of information about how many people clicked an ad. But Google can't tell you anything very useful about the people who clicked, except a pretty good estimate as to where they were when they clicked. Nothing about their age or gender, for instance—which is the basic demographic information that marketers live and die on. (Well, okay, marketers like income data too, when they can get it.)

If you're an experienced marketer, you may be a bit amazed by what Facebook can provide. If you're new to marketing, trust me—you're about to get very lucky in terms of getting accurate and useful data for your advertising work.

Now it's all too easy to read too much into good data. A famous saying in science as well as statistics is, "Correlation is not causation." That is, if there's a huge thunderstorm today and the home team wins its football games tomorrow, it doesn't mean that pregame thunderstorms help the home team.

A lot of marketing is about finding these kinds of correlations and then testing to see if they seem reliable. If you advertise heavily on Friday and get a lot of business on Saturday, did one cause the other? What if the surge of business comes on Sunday—or Tuesday?

Keep an open mind. Treat every occasion on which you advertise, do publicity, or even (shudder) have bad news about your business hit the press, as a fresh opportunity to learn. Keep an open mind and a closed wallet, not the other way around.

Touring the Page Overview in Insights

Facebook Insights provides key information about your Facebook Page in a single place—the Page Overview. For more in-depth information, Insights provides detailed Users and Interactions pages.

Use the Page Overview regularly for a quick update on your Facebook activity. I recommend that you check it daily—at about the same time each day—and note both the results and any related factors, such as your having a sale or promotion, running or stopping a Facebook Ad, school being in or out of session, vacation periods, even the weather. (For a retail operation, for instance, really bad weather might see visits to your Facebook Page go up and check-ins to your Places Page go down.)

There are two main reasons for checking Insights daily rather than, say once a week:

▶ When you see a change in daily activity, you can record what might have contributed to it while it's fresh in your mind.

▶ You have a chance to implement any responses, changes, or new ideas in real time and see the results quickly. You can even mention changes in your stats in a status update.

By using Insights in this way, you'll improve not only your Facebook presence, but potentially your whole business.

TIP: **Export Data from the Page Overview**

The Page Overview is where you export data from, as described in the final section of this lesson.

The best way to get a sense of what Insights can do for you is to take a look at how it actually works. This section takes you on a tour of the Page Overview, explaining the information displayed and showing you how to use the interactive features of Insights. The next two sections describe how to get the most out of the Users and Interactions pages and the additional information they provide.

CAUTION: **You Need 30 Fans to Have Insights**

Insights won't have any content until your page has at least 30 fans. If you don't have Insights for your page yet, use the steps and screenshots in this lesson as an example.

This section provides a tour. In the following sections, I go into more detail about some of the important parts of it—but first, follow these steps to see the Insights stats for your Facebook page:

1. Open your Facebook Home page. Click the **Ads and Pages** link or **See All** if that link is not visible.

2. Underneath the name of your Facebook Page, click the link **View Insights**.

   The Page Overview page of Insights appears.

TIP: **Talking to Other Facebook Page Holders**

Consider asking around for friends and colleagues who have Facebook Pages and will talk to you about their experience with it and using Insights in particular. Sharing "insights" and experiences is a great way to learn.

3. To export data to a spreadsheet or other program, click the **Export** button. In the dialog that appears, choose **Excel (XLS)** or **Comma-Separated (CSV)**. Enter the **Start Time** (which means the beginning date) and the **End Time** (which is the finishing date). Click the **Download** button.

   A CSV file can be easily imported into a word processing document or a wide variety of other programs, whereas an Excel document is usable by Microsoft Excel and a smaller number of other programs.

4. Use the date range drop-down to set the date range to a period that's interesting to you. Click the drop-down menu and then choose the beginning and ending date. Click **Download**.

Figure 14.1 shows a year's worth of stats for Transition San Francisco.

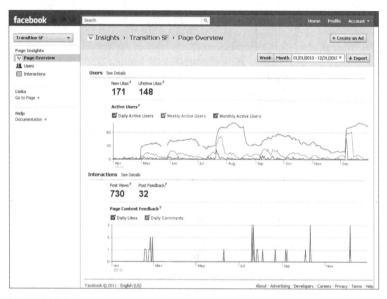

FIGURE 14.1   Insights provides a view of the sustainability group.

> **NOTE: Transition Towns**
>
> Transition San Francisco is part of the international Transition Towns movement for local sustainability. For more information about Transition Towns, visit www.transition.org.

The Page Overview includes summary charts for users and interactions. It's good for a quick overview. Then when you're ready for more detail, the same information—and much more—is available on the detail pages, which are creatively named Users and Interactions.

> **NOTE: It's All About Trends**
>
> If you work with any kind of marketing statistics for a period of time, you'll observe that you end up focusing mostly on trends and possible explanations for them. The absolute numbers often seem less important than trying to figure out what's changing over time

> and why. Giving small amounts of attention to changes in your stats on a regular basis is likely to yield big rewards.

5. Inspect the chart, Active Users.

The Active Users chart shows the number of people who interacted with your Facebook Page. While this is valuable information, you will also want to use other information in Insights to figure out how extensive a typical visit is.

An immense amount of detail about your users appears in the form of a series of graphs. You can get a sense of the functionality of all the graphs by looking at and interacting with the first chart, Active Users, as shown previously in Figure 14.1.

You really have to think carefully to make sense of the statistics. For instance, if you look at the daily view for a week within a given month, the number of monthly active users will steadily increase—not because your page is getting more popular, but because throughout the month, some people are coming to your page for the first time that month. You need to do month-to-month comparisons to get a sense of overall usage trends for the long term.

NOTE: New Likes and Lifetime Likes

Every time someone Likes your page, that's a New Like—and, for the moment, a Lifetime Like. But when someone "Unlikes" your page or closes his Facebook account, he's subtracted from Lifetime Likes. "Lifetime Likes" really means something like "all the Likes you currently have." If you use the drop-down menus to choose a time period that includes the entire history of your page, your New Likes will be all the Likes you've ever gotten; your Lifetime Likes will be either the same number, or something a bit less. Any difference represents people who dropped out. Don't sweat it; having some Unlikes and/or closed accounts is normal.

---

6. Try clicking to set and clear checkboxes and watch as the display updates. Use the Week and Month buttons and the pull-down for changing the date range, as well as the checkboxes, to view the appropriate stats for time periods you're interested in.

Display the stats in ways that make intuitive sense to you and that allow your analytical capabilities to kick in. For instance, Figure 14.2 shows daily statistics for a 2-week period, with the first day a Monday. This focus makes it easy to see trends within a week and how they vary or stay the same across a longer period.

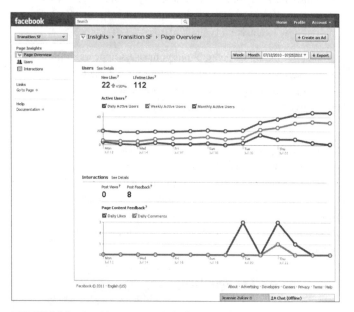

FIGURE 14.2   Looking at a period of a specific number of weeks, for example, allows you to see patterns.

TIP: **Getting Help**

Developer's documentation for Insights is available on all Insights pages. Click the Documentation link on the left-hand side of the page to access it. The documentation is a bit on the technical side, but useful.

---

7. Scroll down and look at the Interactions area, which features the Page Content Feedback graph (as shown in Figure 14.2). Note the Post Views and Post Feedback areas.

Post Views is the number of people who looked at your status updates. Post Feedback is the number of people who gave feedback via either a Like or a comment. In most cases, views will be far higher than instances of feedback.

8. Use the Week and Month buttons and the pull-down for changing the date range to view the number of interactions for various periods. Click the **Daily Likes** and **Daily Comments** checkboxes to show or hide Likes and comments information.

   Interactions are a measure of engagement, and engagement is a kind of Holy Grail for marketers. For more about this, see the section about the Interactions page within Facebook near the end of this lesson.

9. To see the Users page, click the **Users** link in the left-hand rail. To see the Interactions page, click the **Interactions** link just beneath it. To go to your Facebook Page, click the link, **Go to Page**.

   The Users and Interactions pages each begin with the same charts shown here in Figures 14.1 and 14.2. Each page also has additional interactive graphs that give more detail, as well as Demographics (on the Users page only) and Activity (for both). The next two sections describe what's available on the Users and Interactions pages.

Take some time and experiment with this page and with the Users and Interactions pages as well. The Page Overview page is a great way to get a quick update on whether various things you try, or events in the real world, correlate to increases or decreases in your Facebook traffic. You can also compare Facebook activity to sales, right down to the level of day-to-day correlations to find out more about what's working to bring in business. The supporting pages add depth and detail.

Drilling Down on Insights about Users

The Users page in Insights includes interactive graphs with different trendlines that you can show or hide, as on the Page Overview page, plus charts that show breakdowns of demographic or message data. Taken together, they give you a good idea of what's happening on your Facebook Page and should inspire ways to improve it.

The Users page begins with the Active Users graph, which is also on the Overview page (shown previously in Figure 14.2).

The other graphs and charts in the Users page of Facebook Insights are described in this section.

Daily Active Users Breakdown

The Daily Active Users Breakdown graph is a breakdown of what your users actually do while they're actively using your Page. An example for Transition San Francisco is shown in Figure 14.3.

Chart with Post Viewers included

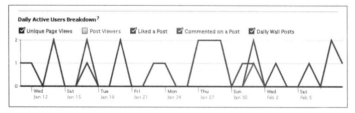

Chart with Post Viewers trendline turned off

FIGURE 14.3 The Daily Active Users Breakdown looks much different with and without the Post Viewers trendline included.

The user activities that Facebook tracks are

▶ **Unique Page Views.** This is how many different pages the user saw. (The page information is broken down by tabs further down on the page.)

- ▶ **Post Viewers.** People who saw one of your posts or status updates. This number is much higher because your status updates go into the News Feed of people who Like your page; people don't have to visit your page to see your posts (though you should frequently invite them to do so). To see the other numbers in more detail, clear the checkbox for Post Viewers so the other lines come into greater relief.

- ▶ **Liked a Post.** The number of users who Liked one of your posts. This is the easiest interaction, so you want to write at least some posts that get a lot of Likes. (This could be a really appealing offer, or personal news such as someone in your business having a new arrival in their family.)

- ▶ **Commented on a Post.** This is more work for users, so it's worth studying posts that get comments to see what's attractive about them—and to do that more in other posts.

- ▶ **Daily Wall Posts.** This should logically be in front of the other post-related categories. It shows the number of Wall posts per day—it's pretty hard for your users to interact with your posts if you don't create any!

New Likes

The New Likes chart "does what it says on the tin"—it shows your new Likes and Unlikes. Look for spikes in both. Spikes in Likes may relate to an ad, promotion, or other activity. Spikes in Unlikes are rare, but they could be a form of silent protest if you fall off in your Facebook activity or post something very unpopular.

The Like Sources area shows where people are Liking your page from. "Page" means the Like button at the top of your Facebook Page. The Like Box describes a little area in the upper right of some pages on Facebook that shows the Likes of your Facebook friends. People often seem to Like things in the Like Box to show a kind of solidarity with their friends—and may be quick to Unlike them if the updates seem annoying.

Users can Unlike your page at any time. They simply click on the little X next to a status update from you and choose **Unlike this page** from the drop-down menu that appears. Don't worry about a few Unlikes, but your new Likes should strongly outnumber your new Unlikes in any given period.

Demographics

The Demographics area, shown in Figure 14.4, is a detailed and potentially very valuable breakdown of whom your users are and where they're coming from. The chart shows the number of men and women in five different age ranges, 18–24 to start, then decade-long groups after that. The groups are split between men and women.

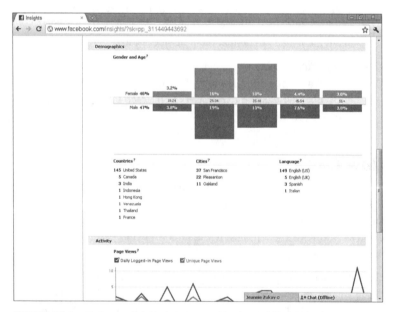

FIGURE 14.4   Get your detailed demographic data while it's hot!

Marketers kill—well, OK, they spend thousands and thousands of dollars—for this kind of information, and what they get is often a mix of facts and estimates. But here Facebook is giving you a very detailed, quite accurate breakdown for free. Do factor in that Facebook users skew female (55:45 in the United States) and younger (heaviest users are mostly under 30). With that in mind, this breakdown may well be fascinating to you.

Note that these percentages don't represent your actual customers or other interested parties, but the ones who are active on Facebook. Because Facebook skews young and female, evaluate how your group compares. For instance, on the Transition page (shown in Figure 14.4), visitors are slightly more male than female and slightly more middle-aged (35 and up) than young (34 and under). This indicates that the real-world group is perhaps even more male and older than the active Facebook users shown in the chart.

Facebook also shows top countries, top cities, and language origins of the page's users. In the example shown in Figure 14.4, it's interesting that nearly 10% of the visitors are from other countries, and fewer than half of those shown in the Cities list are actually from San Francisco. There are a few people whose language is not shown as American English. Don't get too caught up in small numbers like these, though; there are often inaccuracies, and they're not very important, even if true, compared to the big picture.

> TIP: **Keep Your Eyes on the Prize**
>
> Don't get caught up in statistical oddities like the occasional visitor to your page who hails from Tibet. There's some wrong information in Facebook, and odd things really do happen as well. Focus on the bigger picture, like which user groups are largest and how best to meet their needs (and win their business).

Activity—Page Views and Media Consumption

In the Activity area, you see Page Views; Tab Views (a breakdown of where people go when they visit your page); external traffic referrers; and media consumption for photos, videos, and audio files.

The Activity area is shown in Figure 14.5. The major sections are

▶ **Page Views.** This chart has two trendlines—total page views and unique page views. If the same user visits your page four times, that counts as four total page views but just one unique page view. ("Unique page view" really means "unique users who viewed your page.")

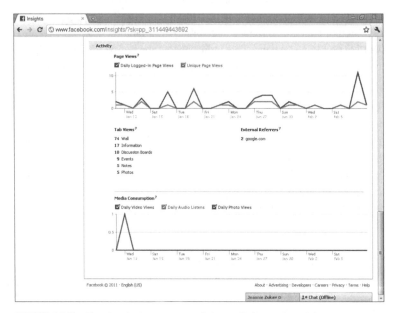

FIGURE 14.5   Facebook draws you a picture of where your visitors go on your page.

▶ **Tab Views.** This chart breaks down where visitors to your page go. As with other data, ignore the small numbers—these can be accidents or the result of someone clicking every tab once. Look at the big numbers; where's most of the traffic? Then think about increasing depth—drawing people to those popular pages, as well as breadth—putting things on the other pages to draw people in.

▶ **External Referrers.** Facebook has a much weaker grasp of this than it does of activity within Facebook; you might need to find other sources for this information, or even ask people how they got to your page.

▶ **Media Consumption.** This chart is great for seeing the results when you put effort into providing videos, audio clips, and photos to your Facebook presence.

Drilling Down on Interactions

The Interactions page within Insights is like the Users page, but it delves into detail about what users do, not just whether they visit your pages.

As mentioned earlier in this lesson, interactions are related to engagement—people identifying personally with you and your business. When people engage with your business online, they're more likely to think of you when they want to buy whatever it is you sell. They're also likely to spend more, tell their friends about you, and so on.

Interactions are hard to get. Usually, many people will look at a piece of information for every one who comments on it. However, it's worth the effort to track comments because they're so closely tied to engagement.

The Interactions page begins with the Page Content Feedback graph, which is also on the Overview page. It's described in a previous section and shown in Figure 14.6.

Page Posts

The Page Posts table shows your top posts from most recent to oldest within the time frame you've chosen. Transition San Francisco's top ten posts for the past year are shown in Figure 14.6.

Insights shows you:

▶ **Message.** Insights shows the first words of the message—and links to the entire message. You can see exactly what people got excited about.

▶ **Posted.** Insights shows the date and time posted. Note that the header has a little triangle on it. Click the header to reverse the sorting order.

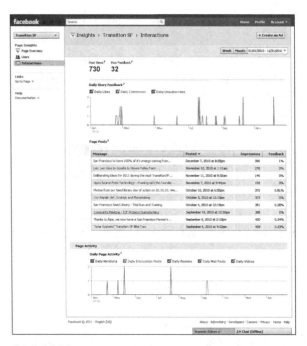

FIGURE 14.6   Insights shows your top posts in the period you specify.

▶ **Impressions.** The number of users who saw the post. These numbers can be pretty impressive for the top posts.

▶ **Feedback.** This is the percentage of people who Liked or commented on the post. Your mileage may vary.

Page Activity

The Page Activity chart shows how your content is reused by others. The trendlines are:

▶ **Mentions.** This refers to visitors mentioning your post in their own status updates.

▶ **Discussion Posts.** Posting to a discussion on your page.

▶ **Reviews.** Writing a review if the opportunity is offered.

- ▶ **Wall Posts.** Mentioning your post on their own post to a friend's Wall.

- ▶ **Photos or Videos.** Uploading photos or videos to your Page.

For many fan pages, this area will be quite skimpy. However, it's worth making an effort to build up your numbers here, as these measurements all reflect a high degree of engagement with your content.

The previous example of Transition San Francisco's page activity (shown in Figure 14.6) reflects a few Mentions and, the last bump on the graph, a Wall Post of our content.

Summary

In this lesson, you learned why tracking your Facebook presence is important and how Facebook can provide you with such accurate demographic information. You also learned how to use the Page Overview in Insights, and how to use the detail pages for Users and Interactions.

This book has taken you on a long journey, from a quick introduction to Facebook all the way to measuring the impact of your Facebook presence on your actual and potential customers. It's amazing how deep those friendly looking Facebook pages can be, in terms of their impact on you and your business. I hope you've enjoyed the journey, and that it contributes to helping you achieve your hopes and dreams.

Index

photos, 77-78

videos, 78-80

website tabs, adapting, 74-75

popularity of Facebook, 9-12

posting

links, 41

photos, 40-41

videos, 41

press mentions from Facebook, 16

privacy settings, changing, 34-39

profile

editing, 31-34

privacy settings, changing, 34-39

profile pictures, adding to fan pages, 102-104

profit, revenue versus, 156

promotion. *See also* advertising

cross-promotions, 192-193

importance of, 183-184

measuring, 185-186

online promotions, 189-191

real-world promotions, 186-189

Q

QR codes, 187

R

real-world promotions, 186-189

relationship status targeting, in Facebook Ads, 166

removing comments, 82

restricting employees' personal Facebook postings, 27

revenue, profit versus, 156

reviews, planning fan pages, 81-83

S

search engine marketing, 163

searching, 30-31, 43-51

security

permissions, installing apps, 51

sharing contact information, 95-96

selecting business names, 87-91

sending

invitations to fan pages, 111-112

spam, avoiding, 191

setting up fan pages

adding apps, 103-104

adding profile picture, 102-104

changing mobile settings, 105-108

entering basic information, 100-102

sharing

contact information, 95-96

on fan pages, 113-118

status updates, 39-42

signing up

for Facebook, 28-29

for fan pages, 91-97

SMS, updating fan pages with, 108

social graph, 128, 148

The Social Network (film), 1

spam, avoiding sending, 191

starting discussions, 122-123

Sams**TeachYourself**

from Sams Publishing

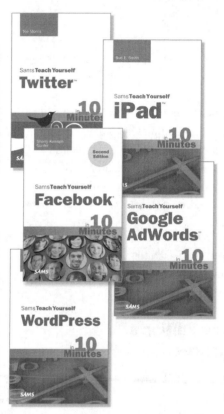

Sams **Teach Yourself in 10 Minutes** offers straightforward, practical answers for fast results.

These small books of 250 pages or less offer tips that point out shortcuts and solutions, cautions that help you avoid common pitfalls, and notes that explain additional concepts and provide additional information. By working through the 10-minute lessons, you learn everything you need to know quickly and easily!

When you only have time for the answers, Sams Teach Yourself books are your best solution.

Visit **informit.com/samsteachyourself** for a complete listing of the products available.

FREE Online Edition

Your purchase of *Sams Teach Yourself Facebook® for Business in 10 Minutes* includes access to a free online edition for 45 days through the Safari Books Online subscription service. Nearly every Sams book is available online through Safari Books Online, along with more than 5,000 other technical books and videos from publishers such as Addison-Wesley Professional, Cisco Press, Exam Cram, IBM Press, O'Reilly, Prentice Hall, and Que.

SAFARI BOOKS ONLINE allows you to search for a specific answer, cut and paste code, download chapters, and stay current with emerging technologies.

Activate your FREE Online Edition at www.informit.com/safarifree

STEP 1: Enter the coupon code: UETREAA.

STEP 2: New Safari users, complete the brief registration form. Safari subscribers, just log in.

If you have difficulty registering on Safari or accessing the online edition, please e-mail customer-service@safaribooksonline.com

Safari
Books Online